What People are Saying About Barry Schumer

"I have known Barry for a long time, and his passion for the Detroit Lions overflows in his latest book. A unique perspective with hope for the fans who feel 2023 is their year."

—Mark Champion
Detroit Lions Broadcaster 1989-2004
Detroit Pistons Broadcaster (30 Years)

"Barry captured the lifetime of frustration 15 years ago, and it culminated with the 0-16 season. I think he hits the nail on the head 15 years later as things have changed in the Lions Den for the better, far better!"

—Sean Baligian
Sportswrap on 760 WJR

"This book embodies the most impactful and insightful writing about the Detroit Lions since, well since the Eisenhower Administration. A must read! BTB!"

—Robert Lincoln
Lions PTSD survivor

"Barry Schumer knows more about the Detroit Lions than anyone I know. He has written about their 'downs,' which have been historically more than their 'ups.' He sees a new breed of Lions under the auspices of Dan Campbell, the coach leading this newly exciting Lions Den. Barry's knowledge of the Lions' statistics is amazing, and he breaks down in fine detail, why these Lions are different and are ready to roar again."

—Stephanie Sanders
Lions Fan

"This book is a must-read for any true Lions fan. Barry's passion, optimism and knowledge of the team and the NFL game is outstanding. Come along for the ride to the Super Bowl!"

—Dr. Len Bayer
Lions Fan

"The Detroit Lions football team is rising from the ashes of history, onto the pages of this book. Readers and fans will have new, exciting memories as our team becomes winners again, as we once were."

—Dr. Jim Weintraub
50 year + Season Ticket holder

"Smart, funny, relatable. Barry is an engaging storyteller."

—Mark Brode
Native Detroiter

"Schumer has combined the harsh realities of the past, with the immense hope for our beloved Lions. This book will inspire, inform and entertain. The future is bright, Lions fans!"

—Howard Morris
Lions Fan

"Barry captures the passions of a community that is both fueled by and empowers the Lions."

—Aaron P. Dworkin
Author, Educator & Social Entrepreneur

"Barry Schumer has meticulously documented the destruction, and now resurrection, of the Detroit Lions football franchise. A great read for all Lions fans."

—Stephen Farkas
Educator and Lions Fan

"I have not enjoyed a book about sports in as long as I can remember, let alone a book about the Detroit Lions. As a female and long-time Lions fan, this sport is not for the faint of heart, and this team, well they have broken my heart many times. Barry's passion and love for this team permeates through his memories and words. Best of all . . . it makes you remember the thrill of competition, and how it felt the first time you watched your team score a touchdown . . . and how we torture ourselves year after year with renewed hope that THIS could be OUR year. This book is witty, smart, and makes you belly laugh out loud. A truly entertaining read . . . but more importantly, it instills hope for a future that could one day include a Super Bowl win, from a team that doesn't know the words 'give up.'"

—Catherine Danhoff
Lions Fan, Saginaw, Michigan

4th Edition

I Don't Believe It...We're Good?

The New

DETROIT LIONS

BARRY SCHUMER

For information about this title or to order other books and/or electronic media, contact the publisher:

Two Sisters Writing & Publishing®
TwoSistersWriting.com
18530 Mack Avenue, Suite 166
Grosse Pointe Farms, MI 48236

ISBN: 978-1-956879-43-8 (Paperback)
ISBN: 978-1-956879-44-5 (eBook)

Printed in the United States of America

All the stories in this work are true.

Cover and Graphic Design: Illumination Graphics.

Author photo: The Schumer Family Collection.

Quotes reprinted with written permission from *The Detroit News* and the *Detroit Free Press.*

Dedication

I dedicate this book to my dear sisters, Marlene and Miriam.
We miss you both. Thanks for believing in me.

Acknowledgments

I would like to thank my publisher Elizabeth Ann Atkins from Two Sisters Writing and Publishing in Grosse Pointe Farms, Michigan. Her expertise in writing and marketing are outstanding. Her personal support and friendship have been key to helping me get over the line with this project.

To Deborah Perdue from Illumination Graphics in Oregon; loved the cover you designed.

To all who provided testimonials for the book, I thank you. Your kind words meant a great deal to me. A special shout-out to Mark Champion, Sean Baligian and Al Rosenberg, who are well known in the Detroit sports community.

Thank you to my family for always believing in me: Zoe, Jason, Marissa, Brandon, Chase, Connor, Lucas, Joanne, Ken, Jen, Chuck, Karen, Lorraine, Jodi, Ron, Talia, Marla, Kayla, Ariella, Sergey, Eve, Ruth, Malvina, Paulina, Dima, Aaron and Afa.

To the memory of Lou Weinstein of Matti's Deli in Dearborn. We had so many conversations about our Lions over the years. Our bet we made in June on the 2023 season, was the last time I saw you. We will miss you.

And a special thanks to Sheila Firestone Ford Hamp, Brad Holmes and Dan Campbell. You have finally provided the hope Lions fans have so desperately needed.

To the 55 men who put on the Honolulu Blue and Silver – go Lions!

A Tribute to Lions Fans

This book is a tribute to the most loyal football fans in the United States . . . Detroit Lions fans. It is remarkable how you have remained loyal over so many years of frustration. And now, Lions fans, it is our time to know what success feels like. Will we see our "boys" play in the Super Bowl soon? I say yes!

It is hard to describe the connection Lions fans have with this team. There is nothing better than waking up on Sundays in the fall and getting ready for game day. In the past, the emotional crash around 4 p.m. could ruin one's weekend. When we finished last season (2022) with an 8-2 record, it revitalized the organization, the team and the fans. This is the most excitement we have had for a season since the days of Barry Sanders.

The key questions to be answered this season are: Will Gibbs and Montgomery be an upgrade at running back? Will Jameson Williams be a game changer? Will Jack Campbell be the stud linebacker the Lions need? Will the new secondary be as good as we think they will be? Will Jared Goff stay healthy? Will Hooker be ready to play, and will he be an adequate backup quarterback? And finally, will Dan Campbell continue to improve with 4th quarter coaching and time management?

So, will I be correct in my prediction of 11-6 this year with a playoff win? Will the Lions be playing in the Super Bowl sometime in the next three seasons by 2025? We will know the answers soon. This is going to be fun!

Contents

Prologue

I met Jim Schwartz at Dan Miller's Lions radio show in Canton, Michigan, shortly after Schwartz became the Lions' head coach in 2009. He was extremely friendly to me and went out of his way to be engaging. I gave him a copy of my original book at his request and signed it, saying, "Welcome to Detroit, Coach, the fans are completely behind you. I believe you will get us to the Super Bowl in three to five years."

The Lions illness and addiction had returned for me. After going through a several-year recovery, I was once again bitten by the hopes and dreams of a fanatical fan. Was I expecting too much?

As I returned to my table that evening, Schwartz called to me.

"Barry," he said, "I hope the next edition of your book is called *I Do Believe It.*"

I replied, "Coach, the fourth edition of the book will be titled, *I Don't Believe It, We're Good?*" That was my hope. Unfortunately, Coach, it's seven years later and I still don't believe it . . .

CHAPTER 1

Are the 2023 Lions As Good As We Think They Are?

IT IS DECEMBER 13TH, 2022 AS I WRITE THIS NEW chapter about our beloved Lions. We just beat the hated division rival Vikings, for the Lions' fifth win in the past six games. We are 6-7 as of today and must win three or four of our last games to make the playoffs. Our odds of making the playoffs are about 20%, mostly due to the tie between the Giants and Commanders a few weeks ago. We have the tiebreaker against both of them.

My third edition was printed in 2014, entitled: *7 Years Later and I Still Don't Believe It . . . Same Old Lions?* The cover has Calvin Johnson's process of the catch fiasco in Chicago in 2010. I have made a pledge to my friends and Lions fans that I would not publish the fourth edition until the Lions won a playoff game. I am breaking this pledge by publishing this edition before a playoff win took place. There is just too much excitement and hope to wait. Of course, all true fans know we have only had one playoff win since 1957. It is all anybody needs to know about the amount of suffering we have endured. That win was in 1991 with Barry Sanders, Chris Spielman, and Eric Kramer.

So, this is the most optimistic I have been about the team in 30 years, since the days of Barry. It appears that Sheila Firestone Ford Hamp, daughter of William Clay Ford, may have finally hit on the best choices for a general manager and head coach: Brad Holmes and Dan Campbell. This organization has never had stable leadership. Without it, winning a championship becomes impossible. I believe Dan Campbell will be the head coach of the Lions for the next 10 to 15 years.

My wife and I took a trip to Israel in 2018. There is a tradition to leave a note to God in the Wailing Wall. I asked in my note for God to protect my family, friends, and clients (I am a psychotherapist); to bring peace between Israel and Palestine; and to please let me see my Detroit Lions play in the Super Bowl before I die. When I told this to our tour guide, he smiled and said, "I think there is a better chance of peace between Israel and Palestine." Lions fans unfortunately have gotten used to this attitude about our football team. No more!

The only painful memory I will bring up here is the Justin Tucker NFL record-setting field goal to win the game for the Ravens on September 26th, 2021. It was classic Lions' "I Don't Believe It" misfortune. The rest of the story is interesting as well.

My buddy had asked me to the game that day. Towards the end of the game, we decided to leave early to beat traffic. I think there were a few minutes left, and we were pretty sure the

Lions had this game won. We put the game on the radio and would listen to history being made. I told my friend Jim that I had the Ravens in my football pool and was going to lose this game. He said to me, "Don't worry, you won't lose your pick."

The Ravens had 4th down and 19, and I again said, "I'm done, there is no way the Ravens win this game."

After they got the improbable 1st down, Jim again said, "Don't worry, you are going to win this pick." The Ravens were then setting up for a 66-yard field goal.

Again, I say, "I'm done, the Lions are going to win, I have no chance." Jim calmly once again said, "Don't worry, you are going to win your pick of the Ravens."

And on replay, it appeared that the Ravens did not get their incomplete pass off on time and should have been penalized five yards. The kick was up, hit the crossbar and got over! It was the longest field goal in NFL history (remember Dempsey's 63 yarder in 1970).

How did my friend Jim believe the Lions would lose this game? How did he so calmly and with such strong conviction predict this loss? Perhaps it was all the disappointments over the years that have "trained" fans to always expect the worst.

The call of the record-setting kick was equally amazing. "It hits the crossbar and bounces over," the announcer said. "Did that just happen? Oh, my goodness, I've never seen anything like it. I'm speechless. And the disappointment for the Lions . . . an agonizing feeling."

✦

My renewed "love affair" with my Lions began this past summer while watching the HBO show *Hard Knocks*. Our Lions were featured. As we watched the Lions training camp, it was amazing to see what goes into preparing these young men to come together as a football team. Seeing the direct instruction of mechanics and understanding of the game, as well as the psychological molding of a team, as they find their "chemistry," was fascinating to watch. We could all see that Campbell had some unique personality traits that might transfer into winning. Hell, I would run through a wall for this guy.

A coach has to both "love" his players while being a disciplinarian as well. He must demand a certain level of effort and performance. But when he sees a young football player having doubts or getting depressed, he must become a "loving father." Campbell seems to possess this "it" factor of a successful coach. He is the most important factor in this team reaching the Super Bowl.

The Lions could easily be 9-4 right now. Their close losses to the Vikings, Seahawks, and Bills could have gone the other way. They also lost the opener to the Eagles (who are now 12-1) 38-35. Our defense struggled early. Receivers were wide open, with no secondary coverage anywhere nearby. The secondary coach was replaced, and coverage has significantly improved. We have developed some very good young players this season.

The Lions have two first-round picks again this year because of the Stafford trade. We will likely pick at five and 15 based on the Rams' poor record this year. I think both picks should be defense; a stud linebacker and another defensive end to help Hutchinson and the pass rush. We have also recently added Jamison Williams, the speedy wide receiver from Alabama who took 10 months to recover from knee surgery. In a sense, we are adding three first-round picks to the team. I would love the top linebacker from Alabama, but this is unlikely.

Detroit is a one-point favorite at the Jets this weekend. There is a new level of respect for the Lions through the NFL and in Vegas. If they can get by the Jets to go to 7-7, they have three winnable games remaining. They are at Carolina (5-8), Home against the Bears (3-10) and at Green Bay (5-8). The Jets and Packers will be a challenge, because they are outdoor cold weather games. At worst, we end up 8-9; at best, 10-7. I actually made two $100 bets with friends that the Lions would go at least 9-8. After their 1-6 start, it was suggested I just send the check. It is amazing that I still have a chance to win these bets.

So, the Lions "illness" has returned to me. My hopes are up. I was so pissed at them after losing an early game, that I moved my Lions picture from my front wall to behind the door of our guest room. My daughter gave me a black and white photo that I framed of Joe Schmitt tackling Jim Brown in Detroit, during the 1957 championship game that we won. As I said here in my earlier editions, this team has not been good for the mental health of its fans.

Jarod Goff has been outstanding this year. He has surprised many of us with his accuracy. Our receivers have been excellent, especially St. Brown. Swift and Williams are an outstanding running back tandem.

Our offensive coordinator, Ben Johnson, has given us one of the best offenses in the League. He is so well thought of, he may get head coaching offers after this season.

I don't think we will "fall apart" and end this season poorly.

It is important to go at least 2-2 the last four games. This momentum needs to build into the draft and next season.

So, our boys beat the Jets, got destroyed by the Panthers in a terrible performance, destroyed the Bears and won the last game against the Packers at Lambeau Field to keep Green Bay out of the playoffs. We finally inflicted some pain to Rogers after all the pain he inflicted on us over the years.

Earlier, on the final day of the 2022 season, Detroit was eliminated from the playoffs when the Seahawks beat the Rams amidst some very questionable officiating. So, I won my two bets predicting the 9-8 record, and the Lions go into the draft, free agency and the 2023 season with great momentum.

The fantastic news after the season ended was Ben Johnson, offensive coordinator, announcing he cancelled his interviews for head coaching positions, and will remain with Detroit. I'm sure the Lions gave him a significant raise for his loyalty. He is a very important piece of the puzzle going forward.

And how about the national television interview with our star running back, Jamaal Williams, after the big Packer win? He cried, dedicating the game ball to his great-grandfather who had died (he broke Barry Sanders' record for Lions rushing touchdowns), and then quickly sobered up and said, "But don't take these tears as a sign of weakness; there will be no more disrespecting the Detroit Lions." It was inspiring. He was amazing. This man is the leader of the Detroit Lions, along with Dan Campbell, of course. They must re-sign him.

In the April draft, the Lions are picking at #6 and #18 in the first round. We will clearly focus on defense. I believe linebacker and secondary help is the priority. We may also take an edge rusher. Tyree Wilson from Texas Tech has been mentioned. Of course, all teams are interested in Will Anderson from Alabama, but he will likely be gone in the first three picks.

So here is my prediction for the next few years for our Detroit Lions: 11-6 in 2023 with a playoff win. And, either in 2024 or 2025, we will watch the Detroit Lions play in the Super Bowl for the first time. No way to know if they win the championship, but they will be there.

Yes, Lions fans, you heard it. Super Bowl! Should I contact a physician because my "Lions illness" has returned?

I have often told my friends that a Lions Super Bowl win would result in the largest city parade Detroit has ever seen. Am I in for another huge let-down? Will our Lions rip my heart out once again? We will know soon.

Since I left you Lions fans in 2014, we have had more failure. After Schwartz went 29-51 over four years, we hired Jim Caldwell. He lasted three years and actually had one of the better coaching stints in Detroit with a 36-28 record. He made two playoff games, but lost both with Stafford. Then began the three years from hell with Matt Patricia, who went 13-29-1.

We have been in the playoffs three times since 1999—2011, 2014, and 2016. All losses. Caldwell made the playoffs two out of three years. He probably should not have been fired. In 2011, the Saints beat us 45-28. In 2014, the Cowboys beat us 24-20. We can never forget the 4th quarter Cowboy penalty flag that was "picked up" because, well, "Jerry Jones requested it." And in 2016, the Seahawks beat us 26-6.

As for General Managers, clearly Chuck Schmidt was the most effective during the Barry years, from 1989-2000. Matt Millen, possibly the worst NFL GM in history, called the shots from 2001-2007. Who can forget him telling his scouts he would pass on Brees; he had Herrington. And we cannot forget the year our fans wore bags over their heads. Martin Mayhew had the honors from 2008-2014. And then Bob Quinn took control from 2016-2020.

And it starts with the Fords. William Clay from 1964-2014. Martha Ford from 2014-2020. And now, Sheila Firestone Ford Hamp is running the show. We may have finally gotten the right Ford. We all thought it would be Bill Ford, Jr., but there must have been a "falling out" between him and his mom.

On January 29th, 2023, the NFC and AFC Championships were played. I predicted the winners would be the Eagles and the Bengals. The first game was won by the Eagles. It was one of the strangest games I had ever seen. The 49'ers basically played the entire game without a QB. The starter was injured on a hit that led to a fumble and turnover. He injured his elbow. The backup QB came in and was terrible. A guy who had been with 13 NFL teams. He was later knocked out of the game with a concussion. So, the starter comes back in (they must have had only two QBs dressed), but was unable to pass the ball, due to his elbow injury. So, he handed the ball off on every play. Any NFL defense that knows you will run every down will destroy you. The game got out of hand at the end where a fight took place as the 49'ers players could not handle their disappointment.

It was sad for the 49'ers fans, the team, and the general

viewing audience. The game was a bust. It would have been very close. This increases my belief that the Lions must get an adequate backup QB. A team is one play away from their season being over.

The second game saw the Chiefs beating the Bengals by three points. It went right down to the end and was an amazing game. Maholms of KC was incredible, playing on a sprained ankle. The final play had him scrambling out of bounds and receiving a late hit by one of the Bengals' best players. A 10-yard personal foul brought the Chiefs to a 45-yard field goal attempt, which they converted. Without the dumb late hit out of bounds, the field goal would have been 55 yards, and likely missed due to strong winds in Kansas City.

The star Bengals defender was devastated as he sat on the bench for a long time after the game. Other players came to console him as he felt the sting of letting his team down. The emotions of the NFL game are incredibly high.

The season came to an end on February 12th, 2023, when the Chiefs became champions of Super Bowl 57, by beating the Eagles 38-35. Interestingly, this was the same score the Eagles beat the Lions by in Detroit in the opening game of the season.

Unfortunately, the refs damaged the ending of this amazing game by calling pass interference on the Eagles with less than two minutes remaining. It was a horrible call that should not have been made. The Eagles would have gotten the ball back, down 3, with over a minute and a half left in the game. They would have had a good shot at tying or winning the game.

However, the other side of it was another terrible call, when the Eagles receiver caught a pass, and clearly fumbled after a nasty hit by the Chiefs. The ball was picked up and run in for a TD by Kansas City. After review, the refs reversed the call, saying it was an incomplete pass because the Eagle receiver did not complete "the process of the catch." Oh, my God, what bullshit. Us Lions fans have understood this since Calvin Johnson's "game-winning catch" in Chicago at the opener in 2010. It was the beginning of "the process of the catch" garbage. So, the Chiefs got screwed out of a TD. I guess the right team won.

In this Super Bowl, it was explained that the player caught the ball, got both feet down and controlled the ball, but did not make a football move going forward. That's because the Chiefs defender knocked the crap out of him!

Officiating has been very problematic in the NFL for many, many years. Yet the popularity of the game keeps growing.

So now, Lions fans wait. We wait for the free agency period in March, and then the NFL draft in April. These next two months are very important to the advancement of Detroit. They need to get a couple solid free agents and must get the draft right. If successful, I stand by my predictions the next three years.

✦

My Lions are playing in Tampa Bay next season! I will definitely get tickets for this one. The schedule does not come out until May 2023. I was very disappointed to hear Brady was retiring. I wanted to see him go against the Lions. But when Fox Sports offers you $375 million to be an NFL analyst on television, with next year off before he starts, it's hard to say no. This was likely a great decision; no more 330-pound guys trying to kill you!

For next season, 27% of the Vegas betting has the Lions winning the NFC! We are not used to this kind of attention. Maybe most of these bets are by Lions fans who have had a relapse of their "Lions illness."

✦

It is March 15th, 2023, and the Lions have had a very successful free agency signing day. We signed an excellent cornerback from the 49'ers, Emmanuel Mosely; another cornerback from the Steelers, Cam Sutton; and a running back from the Bears, David Montgomery. This running back signing likely means the end for Jamaal Williams, who is my favorite player and emotional leader of the team, in my opinion. But this is the "business" of the NFL. Williams wanted a lot of money to stay in Detroit.

Our final two free agents signed were the guard, Graham Glasgow, who played for the Lions early in his career. We also signed a safety from the Eagles, Chauncey Gardner-Johnson. It seems the Lions have had an excellent free agency period.

So now we wait for the next piece of the puzzle, the NFL draft at the end of April. Their first two picks at #6 and #18 are very important. This next season should be very interesting.

Las Vegas odds have come out for the NFL. The over-under number of wins for the Lions is 9.5. That means they think Detroit will win either nine or 10 games. I have gone with 11. As for bets, 47% are on the Lions to make it to the NFC Championship game next season!

It is April 26th, 2023, the day before the NFL Draft. Lions fans always look forward to this. My buddy Al is working the draft for radio from Kansas City. Detroit has already gotten the bad news that our star prospect receiver, Jamison Williams from Alabama, has been suspended the first six games of the year. He made bets from the Lions facility, which is against the rules. He did not bet on football. It seems like a very harsh penalty on the Lions. I could understand a three-game suspension. Williams missed most of his first year recovering from knee surgery. This could definitely affect the draft . . . let's hope they don't use an early pick for a receiver. There are very good ones available in round three and beyond.

April 27th, 2023 . . . our "Super Bowl" has finally arrived. I liked the Lions picks, but many people questioned it: Jahmyr Gibbs, running back from Alabama with their first pick at number 12 of round one. They traded down from #6 to pick up an additional pick. The film on Gibbs is impressive. He is very quick and an outstanding pass receiver. He was the first running back to lead the team in yards, running and passing since 1987. Impressive. An analyst on the NFL Network predicted he would be voted rookie offensive player of the year.

Jack Campbell from Iowa at #18 in the first round. A tough linebacker is exactly what the Lions needed. He is being compared to a Chris Spielman type of guy. I thought it was the Lions most important selection.

Sam LaPorta from Iowa at pick #34 of the second round. A talented Tight End who had a great college career. This is the pick that many people questioned: taking a TE that high in the draft.

Brian Branch from Alabama at #45 of the second round. He is a talented safety that is going to really improve our secondary. He was a solid pick.

Hendon Hooker from Tennessee at pick #68 of the third round. I love this pick. The Lions have gambled the last few years, not having a solid backup QB. You have to have two solid QBs in the NFL, otherwise, you are one injury from your season being over. He is a 6'3", 217-pound QB who can really run and has a cannon for an arm. The film showed him throwing 60-yard bombs with great accuracy. There is only one problem . . . he is coming off ACL surgery that ended his season. He may not be ready to play until November.

Brodric Martin at pick #96 of the third round. A large Defensive Tackle. We will see if he pans out. Colby Sorsdal at pick #152 of round five. He is an Offensive Tackle from William and Mary. And Antoine Green, picked at #219 of the seventh round. He is a wide receiver from North Carolina and looked very good on film. Many experts were surprised he was not picked in an earlier round.

I trust Brad Holmes and Dan Campbell. We will know soon how good these picks are. And now we wait until training camp and the start of the season in September. There is no better time of the year. Patience, Lions fans!

The NFL schedule came out on May 11th for the 2023 season. The Lions open on the road at Kansas City on national television September 7th. It is an honor playing the Super Bowl champs, earned by Detroit with their 8-2 record at the end of last season. I think we have a very favorable schedule. The hardest three games are at the Chiefs, at the Ravens, and at the Chargers.

I predict we go 8-0 at home, and 4-5 on the road for 12-5. And of course, getting that first playoff win since 1991. The Lions cannot go backwards this year. An 8-9 or 7-10 season would be a complete disaster. Ideally you win the best record in the NFC and get two playoff games at home on the way to the Super Bowl.

I am looking forward to going to see our boys in Tampa Bay on October 15th. We will be at our winter home just before that game. We should be able to win that one without Brady.

✦

Enjoy the 2023 season, Lions fans. It is the most important one we have had in many years. You never know what can happen due to injuries, difficult weather games, and late-game coaching decisions. From September into January, we will be glued to our televisions on Sundays and the other national game days. From September 7th until January 7th, we will have great entertainment. We are hoping that the Lions are in a playoff game either January 14th or 21st. And by the way, Super Bowl 58 will be in Las Vegas on February 11th, 2024.

CHAPTER 2

7 Years Later and I Still Don't Believe It!
2012: What Happened?

IT HAS BEEN SEVEN YEARS SINCE I WROTE THE FIRST edition of *I Don't Believe It; Memories of a Detroit Lions Fan.* I wrote the book as an unbelievably frustrated fan at the end of the Millen era. Today, as I write this chapter, I am again disappointed with the progress of the organization these past seven years.

When one is objective about the Lions, several important questions must be asked. First, was it realistic to expect a major turnaround with a first-time head coach and general manager? Second, will William Clay Ford ever be an owner that will watch his team play in the Super Bowl? The answer to both questions is no.

Let's first look at GM Martin Mayhew. He is clearly a professional person and seems to be a very nice guy. But his draft record has not matched his personal qualities. The gamble on Jahvid Best appears to be a bust. He has drafted two wide receivers in the second round the last two years in Young and

Broyles while we have had one of the worst secondaries and defenses in the League the past four years. Young was cut from the team because I believe he was a punk, and Broyles tore his knee for the second straight year. Broyles has great potential if he can recover. Riley Reiff was our top pick this year, but did not start on a weak line. It is clear that the two weakest parts of this team are the offensive line and the secondary. Yet, little has been done to shore up either one.

Now, let's look at head coach Jim Schwartz. His rise from 2-14 in 2009 to 6-10 in 2010 and 10-6 in 2011 has been impressive. He took the team to their first playoff game since 1999. We can talk later about the 45-28 thrashing they took from the Saints in that playoff game. And here we are as I write, at 4-5 after nine games in the 2012 season. We are facing the Packers at home this weekend. I am not optimistic; I am predicting a 17-point win by the Packers. I have been wrong before and I hope I am wrong again. You just get the feeling that the team is about to unravel. I believe they will win no more than three additional games this year and be 7-9 at best. It is very possible they could go 5-11. If this happens, it will be considered a major setback.

If they have a losing season, which seems sure, I'm not sure how Schwartz can have any credibility if he doesn't make some major changes, most likely by firing one or both coordinators. They might also fire the special teams coach after the "I don't believe it" NFL all-time record of four returns for touchdowns in back-to-back games with the Titans and Vikings.

If the Lions had an active owner, they would likely insist on a major personnel change, and Schwartz's job might be on the line. But we don't, so you never know what might happen. I believe the Lions may not be able to move forward until Bill Ford, Jr. becomes the owner. He has been the CEO of Ford Motor Company—he will not accept mediocrity.

I went to see the Lions in Arizona in November of 2007. The Lions came into that game with an impressive 6-2 record. I was holding a large banner saying, "I Don't Believe It We're Good!" I'm not sure it ever got on TV. The day before the game, I was at the hotel when the team was getting off the bus. One person shook my hand as he walked by—head coach Rod Marinelli. I appreciated him doing that. After I shook his hand, Marinelli went 1-23 the rest of his Lions career. I have told friends that it was my fault and they have asked me never to shake Jim Schwartz's hand. Too late!

As you all know, the 2008 season will go down in infamy. I doubt another NFL team will match our imperfect 0-16 record in my lifetime. Jim Rome was hilarious as he begged the Lions to "man down" and finish the job. He had always dreamed of a team running the table in reverse. He got his wish.

Marinelli said some strange things as the head coach of the Lions. Fans will remember when he said, "My shovel is sharp; my pick is sharp," referring to his work ethic at a press conference. He also said, "I believe in the invisible." He had run-ins with some of the sports reporters covering the team: Tom Kowalski said, "Whatever," after a Marinelli answer once, and Marinelli said, "Whatever to you," in response.

After the Lions were 0-15 in 2008, *Detroit Free Press* sports columnist Rob Parker resigned in the midst of controversy after he asked Marinelli, "Do you wish your daughter would have married a better defensive coordinator?" His son-in-law, Joe Barry, was the defensive coordinator of the Lions.

Since history was made, I must include the scores of all 16 games beginning September 7th, 2008 and ending December 28th, 2008:

Atlanta 34-21
Green Bay 48-25
San Francisco 31-13
Chicago 34-7
Minnesota 12-10
Houston 28-21
Washington 25-17
Chicago 27-23
Jacksonville 38-14
Carolina 31-22
Tampa Bay 38-20
Tennessee 47-10
Minnesota 20-16
Indianapolis 31-21
New Orleans 42-7
Green Bay 31-21

The 2012 season began after a bizarre off-season that saw several players arrested. Several were for drug issues, DUIs, and one that involved pulling a gun on someone. We went into the season after a very chaotic off-season. We opened the season with a home win against St. Louis in the last 10 seconds of the game. Our 2012 Lions have had the inexplicable habit of playing very poorly the first half of games and even through the third quarter. We lead the NFL in fourth-quarter scoring. This is a tribute to Matt Stafford, who is a great comeback quarterback, and due to the fact that we are usually behind entering the last quarter.

We lost at San Francisco and were never really in the game. We then lost in overtime in Tennessee in a shoot-out. This one included two returns for touchdowns and a fumble returned for a TD. We lost when Shaun Hill bobbled a snap on a QB sneak on fourth and 1. They passed up the tying field goal, which I had no problem with. We continued our special team's circus show the next week at home against the Vikings. Again, we gave up two returns off kicks for touchdowns. Another NFL first—no team has ever given up four kick or punt returns for TDs in back-to-back games in the history of the League. I love records! We then won a big game at the Eagles, who proved to have an underperform-ing team this year. We lost in Chicago on Monday night. We beat the Seahawks on a last-second touchdown similar to the opening win against the Rams. We beat a bad Jaguar team on the road and for the first time we led throughout the game. We have only led at halftime once or twice this year. And last week we lost in Minnesota and were never really in the game.

The terrible starts and the inconsistency clearly point to coaching. I am not a big fan of our offensive coordinator, Scott Linehan. When I watch Calvin Johnson I feel it is a repeat of watching Barry Sanders and his wasted career in Detroit. I say "wasted" in the sense of any chance at a championship. At least Barry got to play in one NFC championship game, even though we were destroyed by the Redskins in 1991.

Calvin Johnson is a special athlete who comes around very rarely. When he was drafted in 2007, my buddy wanted them to pick Joe Thomas, who has become one of the best offensive linemen today. It's hard to know who would have been better for Detroit. It sure is fun watching Calvin, but we know how important great offensive linemen are to the game today.

Now let me add to the first 20 "I Don't Believe It" moments I wrote about in the first edition of the book. Let's start with Ndamukong Suh's stomping incident on national television on Thanksgiving Day against the Packers in 2011. I have already mentioned the four-kick returns for touchdowns in back-to-back games, which is an NFL record. How about Fairley and Leshoure getting arrested for marijuana possession a few weeks apart in the off season? And, of course, who could forget Calvin Johnson not completing the process of the catch in the opener in Chicago in 2010? The apparent touchdown in the last minute of the game against the Bears would have won it for Detroit. My buddy Larry was so upset, he left my place immediately. I had never seen him that angry. In 2012, we saw Stefan Logan take a knee at the 4-yard line on a kickoff against Chicago in the last minute of the game. I think he was supposed to let it go into the end zone for a touch back.

On September 13th, 2010 read, Sean Brennan of the *Daily News* wrote that during the game in Chicago, Calvin Johnson and the Detroit Lions were "robbed" as they totaled 21 losses at away games.

Oh, the agony. In Chapter 10, The Top 20 I Don't Believe It moments since 1970, this one becomes number three.

And now we come to the Thanksgiving game of 2012 against the Houston Texans. What can anyone say about this one? It was bizarre even for the Lions. The "I Don't Believe It" moment was the 81-yard run for a touchdown by Houston that was not a touchdown. Replay clearly showed he was down, but he popped up and kept running. There was no whistle. The refs blew this one big and made the NFL look foolish. Schwartz reacted quickly by throwing a challenge flag. Wrong move! Neither Schwartz nor any of the other coaches knew of a ridiculous rule that prevented the refs from reviewing the play after Schwartz threw the challenge flag. You also need to wonder why the defense did not chase the runner since they did not hear a whistle. I think they were in shock since it was rather obvious to everyone on the field except the refs that the player was down.

So that was the lowlight from the game. But there was more. Twice in the final few minutes of the game the Lions had 3rd down at the Houston 36-yard line. A field goal would have put them up 10. Both times they dropped Stafford back to pass, and both times he was sacked to take them out of field goal range. How stupid can the coaches be? The Lions were inside Houston's territory six times in the second half and overtime, where they didn't score a point! Of course, this wasn't enough torture for Lions fans and players. We had to watch Houston narrowly miss an overtime field goal attempt from 51 yards and then watch Detroit hit the right goal post from 47 yards that would have won the game. Linehan and Schwartz decided to make the attempt on 3rd down. This is usually done when the field goal is a "chip shot" from 30 yards or less. It is obvious they should have used 3rd down to gain five more yards, or possibly a first down.

This game is more proof of poor coaching. I felt really bad for the players who played their hearts out. I have wanted the offensive coordinator Linehan fired for some time now. Schwartz deserves one more year to prove himself. He is a very likable guy who seems to have the respect of his players. But any thoughts about change are futile, because William Clay Ford is an intensely loyal owner and has a hard time letting people go.

I have felt for years that the Lions will never win under his ownership. I have felt guilty, as there have been days after brutal Lions losses that I have actually wished for his demise. I believe his son, Bill Ford, Jr., is more likely to bring us a winner than his father.

I have only wanted two people to die in my lifetime: Saddam Hussein and Osama bin Laden. Most people would understand that. I'm sure Mr. Ford is a very nice man; I no longer wish for his demise. I remember his son, Bill Ford, Jr., telling the story of his father this past kickoff luncheon, saying that when he first bought the team, his dad couldn't sleep for the few nights before the Sunday game. He would pace the floors, excited for Sunday to come. Maybe it is just that difficult for an owner to put the pieces together in an NFL organization that results in a Super Bowl win.

On the Friday after the Thanksgiving game, I noticed the frame of my Lions newspaper interview about my book was slightly separating. I didn't make much of it until the next day when I heard a crash in my library. The frame had completely separated and the glass had broken.

Was this a sign from God? What was I to make of this? Was it just a random occurrence? I think it means more tough days ahead as a Lions fan, or could it mean that I should go forward with the third edition of the book?

So, we move to game 12 for the Lions at home against the Colts and rookie sensation QB Andrew Luck. The Lions lose this one in creative fashion, giving up a 12-point lead with less than three minutes to go. The Colts scored two TDs in the final two minutes and 38 seconds of the game. The good news is that we set another record as the first team in 32 years to lose three consecutive games with the lead at the two-minute warning. Our records always seem to be the wrong kind.

This came down to a 3rd down and 5 on the Colts side of the 50. Instead of letting your franchise QB win the game with a first down with less than two minutes left, they ran a sweep left for no gain. The brilliant coaches decided to put it in the hands of our defense with a minute and 18 seconds left. The comedy of the next 78 seconds began with a 25-yard punt that went out of bounds at the 25-yard line. And then Gunther Cunningham's prevent defense went into action. The defensive line was very tired at this point and had limited pressure on the Colts' QB. There was also no spy on Luck to prevent him from getting out of the pocket. The Colts got down to the Lions' 11-yard line with no time outs and 18 seconds left. Any veteran Lions fan knew it was over at that point. And then the Lions surprised us—they stopped three consecutive passes in a row and got the clock down to four seconds. But the Lions remembered their history and allowed the winning TD as the clock expired. Luck broke containment and was able to throw a three-yard pass to the five-yard line and the receiver walks into the end zone virtually untouched. It looked like the defense sent seven players to cover the end zone—they forgot the middle of the field was wide open. And once again, fans said, "I Don't Believe It!"

The only good news from this one was that Calvin Johnson had 13 catches for 171 yards and is well in reach of Jerry Rice's all time reception total of 1,850 yards set in 1995. Calvin reaching this record is the only thing I care about the rest of the season.

The Lions traveled to Green Bay where they have not won since 1991. It is the longest losing streak to the same team on their home field in NFL history. Another distinction for the Detroit Lions.

This one was a classic. I told my friends that I thought they would go with plan 52 in the book *100 Ways to Lose an NFL Game*. That plan calls for Detroit to dominate the Packers for the first quarter into the second, and then begin the dismantling towards another loss. The Lions were the sharpest they had been all season the first 20 minutes of the game. Two drives resulting in touchdowns. Then the first signs of trouble began. We were flagged 15 yards for excessive celebration after the second TD. With the shortened kick off, the Packers were able to kick a field goal and bring the score to 14-3. And then the big moment in the game: the ball slipped out of Stafford's hand as he was about to throw. It led to a fumble recovery and return for a touchdown. Instead of driving and making the score 21-3, it became 14-10 in a blink of an eye.

We lost the game 27-20. I turned it off with three minutes to go when Stafford and the offense went 4 and out with no first downs. The Packers outscored us 27-6 after we had gotten off to the 14-0 lead. The good news was that Calvin Johnson had over 100 yards receiving and is on his way to breaking Jerry Rice's all-time receiving record for a season.

Now we watch this Sunday as the Lions play the Arizona Cardinals who have lost nine in a row after starting the season with four straight wins. They lost last week to Seattle 58-0! I predict the Lions will lose this game. My friends believe the Lions have more talent and will win the game. This is set up to be a classic Lions moment. If they lose out like I believe they will, the Lions will have a chance at the third or fourth pick in the 2013 draft in April.

My buddy told me that he would walk back to Detroit if the Lions lost in Arizona. I texted him in the fourth quarter and wished him good luck in his travels and that I would see him some time in February after his 1,800-mile trek! One of our sports personalities, Jamie Samuelsen, reported that his six-year-old son said "never again" after this one! A smart boy.

The Lions went on to lose their last game against Chicago—their eighth in a row—to finish 4-12. I didn't make an effort to see it as I was in Florida with my wife.

CHAPTER 3

Do the Lions Still Stink?
Let's Hope Not (2007-2013)

MY BUDDY GAVE ME A REMARKABLE STAT ABOUT THIS year and the Jim Schwartz record over four years with Detroit. His record is 4-20 against the NFC North rivals Chicago, Minnesota, and Green Bay. During this same period, Detroit is in the worst position of the four teams regarding salary cap room. The top team is $13 million under the cap to sign their own and other free agents, and the Lions are $1 million over the cap.

So not only do we end up last in the North division, but are also in the worst financial shape to improve. This organization is so inept, it is hard to imagine. And then we hear that the coach of the Bears, Lovie Smith, is fired after winning 10 games this year. Next up, the draft in April.

It is Sunday, February 3rd, 2013. Super Bowl Sunday! The 47th time this classic will be played without my beloved Detroit Lions. The first Super Bowl in 1966 was played two years after William Clay Ford purchased the Lions. We are only one of two established teams never to appear in the big game—the other one being Cleveland. Houston and Jacksonville are the other two teams never to appear.

I had quite a personal scare a month ago after complications from surgery, in which I almost died at age 57. It gives you a new perspective on life. I told my buddy that it just wouldn't have been right if I died before William Clay Ford, who is in his late eighties. Luckily, I am still here and have a shot to see my Lions play in the Super Bowl before I die. This is tops on my bucket list.

The 49'ers and the Ravens are in today's big game. The Harbaugh brothers going against each other—the NFL could not be happier from a marketing perspective. I think the 49'ers will win, but you never know.

I told my good friends that I will only follow the Lions with a casual interest this next season if one of the coordinators is not fired. Both coordinators are coming back after a pathetic 4-12 season. Another "I Don't Believe It" for the Lions. The Ravens, playing in Super Bowl 57, didn't hesitate to fire their offensive coordinator in the middle of this season after three losses in a row! It is amazing how little Ford, Sr. expects from this team, his head coach, and his general manager.

I was 10 years old when the first Super Bowl was played. I have seen one playoff win from the Lions in my lifetime. I do not count the 1957 championship because I was two years old and not yet a fan. All of my hopes for this team that I love rest with Bill Ford, Jr. I hope he comes through for me and the millions of die-hard Lions fans all over the country. Time will tell.

It is March 11th, 2013, and tomorrow is the first day free agents can be signed. It is critical that the Lions sign two starters. The draft is in six weeks and must result in two more starters.

What a surprise! The Lions had a very good free agent signing period. We signed Reggie Bush (to replace the concussed Jahvid Best). The best signing might have been the safety Glover Quin from Houston. We re-signed Chris Houston, our best corner. And we signed a good DE from Seattle, Jason Jones, who played his high school and college football in Michigan. We also signed our safety Delmas (let's hope he can play half a season without injury). We lost Cliff Avril as expected.

The other big news was the retirement of our left tackle, Jeff Backus. He started for us for 12 years and only missed one game—very impressive. I met him at a hotel in Chicago last year; he is a great guy and very professional. We have now lost three of our five starters on the offensive line from last year. Will the Lions be smart enough to use their first or second round pick for a starting offensive lineman? If they do not, Stafford and Bush will be running for their lives.

Draft day 2013 is April 25th. My buddy and I have a tradition to golf in the afternoon, have dinner, and then tune into the draft coverage. I believe that the Lions will win six to eight games this year with a poor draft; with a good draft (offensive lineman and linebacker with the first two picks) they may win eight to 10 games. The main reason I am not optimistic about this season is the very difficult schedule and the fact that we return with both our coordinators; one or both deserved to lose their job after last season.

I did some research on the NFL playoffs and our Detroit Lions. Obviously, it's bad news, but just how bad? Here are the top 10 organizations based on number of playoff appearances (through 2013):

Dallas (58)

Pittsburgh (54)

Green Bay (48)

New York Giants (48)

San Francisco (47)

Minnesota (46)

L.A./St. Louis (43)

Oakland (43)

New England (41)

Washington (41)

The top winning percentages in the NFL playoffs are:

W/L/Win %

Green Bay 30/18/62.5

Pittsburgh 33/21/61.1

San Francisco 28/19/59.6

New England 24/17/58.5

Oakland 25/18/58.1

Dallas 33/25/56.9

Washington 23/18/56.1

Denver 18/17/51.4

N.Y. Giants 24/24/50.0

Miami 20/20/50.0

Other teams with solid winning percentages (50.0) in the playoffs:

Baltimore 14/7/66.7

Carolina 6/4/60.0

Houston 2/2/50.0

Now we come to our beloved Lions. They have won seven

playoff games, and lost 11. That is a .389 winning percentage. No surprise here. And of the seven playoff wins, six were between 1935 and 1957. The Lions are 1-10 in the playoffs (through 2013) since 1957. William Clay Ford made the playoffs for the first time in 1970 after buying the team in 1964. This was the famous 5-0 loss against the Cowboys. The Lions did not make the playoffs again until 1982 (12 years later). So, Ford made the playoffs once in his first 17 years—not a great start. We made the playoffs six times from 1991 to 1999—can you say Barry Sanders? And after Barry, we have made the post-season just once in 13 years.

There are five teams with a lower winning percentage in the playoffs than the Lions: San Diego 10/16 (.385); Atlanta 7/12 (.368); Kansas City 8/14 (.364); Cleveland 11/20 (.355); and Cincinnati 5/11 (.313).

The William Clay Ford record is a complete failure. One play-off win in 48 years of ownership is simply pathetic. We will see if things change after Mr. Ford passes.

Jason Hanson has retired. He holds the record for the most 50+ yard field goals in NFL history. He was an excellent kicker and a professional. His retirement surprised me since he was in good shape at age 42. I thought he would kick until age 45. He did have some injuries the past few years that may have been part of his decision. I think he was just tired of losing—being a Lion can be hard to sustain.

Scott McEwen has been the director of college scouting for the Lions the past 25 years. Recently, the 32 NFL teams were rated for their drafts since 1993. The Lions were ranked number 31. How can someone keep such an important position on a team for this length of time with such a poor record of drafting? There is only one explanation—he must be one of Mr. Ford's buddies.

The NFL draft is only three days away—it is the Super Bowl for Lions fans. I am hoping they get one of the three top offensive linemen available—I especially like Lane Johnson from Oklahoma. The Lions will likely take a defensive lineman; I wouldn't be shocked if they took a wide receiver.

Our schedule came out last week and it looks pretty tough. We open at home against the Vikings and close the season against them on the road. We play at Arizona and Washington, where we never win. We play at Green Bay in October, which is great for weather—only problem is we haven't won there since 1991—amazing! I am hoping to travel to Chicago in week 10 to see our Lions in the beginning of November. We had a great time when we went there two seasons ago, even though the Lions were destroyed and Stafford threw four interceptions with his broken finger. My guess at this point is that we go 8-8.

With the fifth pick in the 2013 NFL draft, the Detroit Lions select Ziggy Ansah, defensive end from Brigham Young. He is described as a physical freak at 6' 7" and 270 pounds who runs 4.7 seconds from 40 yards. NFL media say he is the best athlete they have ever seen. He is a bit of a project since he has only played football for two years. He may become a pro bowler or could be a total bust. I was okay with the pick since all three offensive tackles were taken in the first four picks—just the Lions' luck! It was funny when, during an interview, Ansah said, "We will be back to New York for the Super Bowl." Wasn't that cute? The young man has no idea what just happened to him; when the Lions pick you in the draft, it is likely the end of your career! We picked a solid cornerback from Mississippi State, Slay, with the second pick and a huge guard from Kansas State, Wolford, in the third round. The guy is 6' 3" and 335 pounds. We picked another defensive end in the fourth round, a punter with the fifth pick, and finished with a receiver and a linebacker.

I really liked getting the punter Sam Martin from Appalachian State. He averaged 46 yards a punt in college and kicked 25 out of bounds inside the 20. I believe a great punter is a very important part of a team, as they can totally change field position.

I think it was a good draft for the Lions, but the key will be just how good and how soon Ansah can start. Our Super Bowl is over; it was a great three days. It was fun seeing Barry Sanders make the first pick and hear that he was selected to be on the cover of the video game Madden 25.

So now we wait. We wait for training camp in July, the preseason in August, and then the magical opening day in September. Until then, my friends and I try get in as much golf as possible.

It's May 7th, 2013, and my friend just let me know that our second-round pick, the corner back Slay, will have to have knee surgery. He will miss the entire rookie training camp, but should be ready for the team camp in July. Where have we seen this before? How about last year when they took the wide receiver Broyles who was coming off knee surgery with the second pick. Broyles went on to tear his other knee halfway through the season. Let's hope Slay is not injury prone; you can only guess wrong on second round picks so long (remember Jahvid Best) before you assure continued losing.

Matt Shepard had an amazing stat on his WDFN 1130 show today, June 4th, 2013. Since 1933, the Pittsburgh Steelers have had only eight 10-loss seasons. The Detroit Lions have had ten 10-loss seasons since 2001. I don't believe it! You don't realize just how bad it is until you examine the numbers closely.

The good news today is that Bill Ford, Jr. addressed the press in Allen Park at the Lions' training facility. He was optimistic about the team and the direction for next season. He was sounding a lot like an owner! The word is that his father has been ill recently. Maybe he has decided to turn the reins over to his son so he can have the pleasure of watching him run the team before he dies. Bill Ford, Jr. is the last hope I have to see a winning Lions team in my lifetime. Wouldn't it be great if he could accomplish what his father could not?

I heard an interesting story about William Clay Ford recently. When he was at Ford Motor Company, he asked a friend there if he wanted to become the General Manager of his Detroit Lions football team. The man told him he didn't know anything about football. Ford's response was, "We'll figure it out together." Need I say more?

It is July 26th, 2013. The Lions are opening their training camp. The long wait from January through July is finally over. There will be more and more Lions talk on sports radio shows over this next month until their preseason opener on August 9th against the Jets.

Since the Tigers will be in the race for the World Series, they will share the spotlight with the Lions through October. But even if the Tigers make it to the World Series, you will see the Lions dominate sports radio in Detroit in September when the regular season begins at home against the Vikings.

I went to the Lions practice this past week. The place was packed! The eternal hope of a new season filled the air. We had a great spot around the 30-yard line, and Calvin Johnson was going through the receiver drills right in front of us. I have seen him before, but it is really amazing to see this guy up close. He is huge and a physical marvel. I have no idea how a 5'9" cornerback could possibly cover him. I guess they can't, as indicated by Calvin breaking Jerry Rice's record last year.

We were standing next to two guys who were in their late 20s or early 30s. I was amazed how optimistic they were about the team and, at the same time, how unrealistic they were. They were very protective of their hometown heroes. When I had concerns about the offensive line, they pointed out that they were in the top five in fewest sacks last year. Their stat was off, due to the fact that Stafford got rid of the ball in under three seconds most of the time.

The belief that Ziggy Ansah was looking great and would probably start was wrong. I have heard that he is not ready to start at defensive end just yet. The main point here was the excitement they had for the team this year. When I went to the preseason opener against the Jets, which we won 26-17, I was struck again with the unrealistic hope and optimism fans have. I described the upcoming third edition of this book and some of the concerns I had for this season (coaching, offensive line, linebackers), and the fans sitting near me in Ford Field let me have it. They were not in the mood to hear anything negative about their heroes. Several fans around me were predicting a 10- or 11-win season. The Lions illness is at its most potent level in August before the season starts. It is as though the 4-12 season last year never happened!

This hope in July is a universal happening for fans with all the NFL teams. But in Detroit it is even more intense. When you have been disappointed over the last 55 years, the hope for a winner becomes even more intense.

The first play at practice had Stafford faking a hand-off to Reggie Bush and throwing to Pettigrew on the other side of the field. There wasn't a defensive player within 20 yards of him. I said, "I recognize that defense." The die-hard fans were not amused.

I called into the Terry Foster show on 97.1 The Ticket recently. His question to fans was, "Is it fool's gold that he thinks the Lions will contend for a playoff spot this year?" When I got on the air, my answer was yes. I said that I doubted the Lions would win more than eight games this year. I told Foster that I thought we had some very good players, but I had no confidence in the coaching staff. I said that if Bill Cower or Tony Dungy were our coach, we might win 10 or 11 games. At that point, Foster began to defend Schwartz and describe the changes he has seen in him since he first came to Detroit four years ago. He agreed that if they have another poor season, there would have to be major changes. I also pointed out after he said he thought the Lions could go 3-3 in the North division, even though Schwartz had a record of 4-20 in the North his first four years.

I made a bet with a guy I know from my friend Jim's golf club (Travis Pointe Country Club) in Ann Arbor. I bet Rob two years ago that the Lions would win 10 or more games and go to the playoffs. I had returned to my optimistic, hopeful fan state, and I guessed right as they went 10-6 and made it to the playoffs. I won the $250 bet. Since I was not in the member-guest tournament at the golf club last summer, I did not see Rob to either collect or go double or nothing on the bet. This summer was a repeat; I was not able to get an invite from a club member for the tournament. But I employed the services of my friend Jim to act as my agent with Rob. I told him we would go double or nothing on the $250 he owed me and that he could pick either eight wins or less, or nine wins or more this season for the Lions. I gave him the choice because Rob gave me the choice two years ago. I was hoping that he would go with the nine wins or more and he did!

I am confident that Rob will owe me $500 by the middle of November. I do not see the Lions winning more than eight games this year with a tough schedule, a new offensive line, and coaches who have not proven themselves. After the bet two years ago, Rob was promoted to CEO of his advertising firm. I plan on collecting on the bet this year.

After I wrote the second edition of this book in 2007, a fan told me a great story about the Lions. She remembered watching Lions games with her grandfather and how upset he would get about some of the losses. After one particularly frustrating loss at the end of the game, she remembered him getting so upset that he grabbed the TV, pulling the plug out of the wall, and he threw it through the living room window, breaking the glass and hearing it crash on the cement below. Her grandmother was not very happy about this and he slept on the couch for a while after that.

This is a great example of the passion fans have for our Lions and the NFL game. Our team can make us crazy! There are many stories like this. I watched a game with my friend Mark a few years ago. The Lions were terrible at Philadelphia and were losing by three touchdowns in the first half. Mark lost it, swore at the TV, and finally shut it off. We went outside to throw a football around and we never returned to the game. After that, Mark began giving me his Lions stuff he had gathered over the years; his Lions gym shoes, a team mirror, a Lions doll where you could pull off body parts, a Lions pillow, etc. He was trying his best to stop being a fan, but I know he still cares about the team.

My friend Anne told me that she has to flip back and forth between two football games on Sundays because she is too nervous to watch the entire Detroit game. She gets a stomach ache before Lions games most Sundays. I told you that being a Lions fan is not good for your physical or mental health!

The Lions lose 24-6 at Cleveland in their second exhibition game of the year. They looked pretty bad. It is amazing how different this team looks without Calvin Johnson, who did not play because of a bruised knee. The offense could not get going; the defense looked bad, and the special teams were terrible. We had two personal fouls by Bush and Suh, reminding us of the lack of discipline Lions players have shown over the years.

Drew Sharpe of the *Detroit Free Press* wrote the next day that, "August is important to build the confidence of the players as well as the legions of faithful fans who are loyal despite the miserable history of this franchise." Well said, Mr. Sharpe, well said!

Now let's remember that the win-loss record in the preseason means nothing. We were 4-0 in 2008 when we went 0-16 during the season. But there are major concerns that are obvious at this point. The acronym COOL describes my concerns well: Coaching, Ownership, Offensive Line, and Linebackers.

The Lions announced that Bill Ford, Jr. was named to the Broadcast Committee of the NFL. There are 10 owners on this committee and it is supposed to be an honor to be a member. My buddy feels this is a clear sign that Bill Ford, Jr. is now in charge as his father struggles with medical issues. This committee is responsible for growing the game and making deals to expand broadcast avenues for the League. Bill Ford, Jr. has a proven successful background in business as the CEO of the Ford Motor Company.

I saw Jim Schwartz in his press conference after the game. I feel bad for him. He has clearly worked as hard as he can to bring a winning team to Detroit. But hard work in professional sports does not necessarily transfer into winning. He has been rewarded with the stature of being a head coach in the NFL—not easy to achieve. He has also been rewarded financially; I'm not sure what Schwartz makes, but I'm sure it is at least a million a year. But his record of 22-42 is not good. His record of 4-20 in the North conference is even worse. This is his fifth year—how can he keep his job if he doesn't win at least eight games? With Mr. Ford, you just never know. As I said earlier, Schwartz is an amazingly nice guy. He was fantastic to me when I met him in 2009 at a radio show. Sadly, we may be looking at the end of the Jim Schwartz era in Detroit. I hope he pulls out of it; I really thought he was going to be a good head coach who would be here for 20 years.

Out of the 10 teams with the worst record in the NFL last year, nine had a major firing from their staffs. Guess which team made no changes in upper management? Of course, it was our Lions. The other nine teams either fired their General Manager, head coach, or their offensive or defensive coordinators. We have seen this pattern since William Clay Ford became the owner in 1964. His loyalty to his employees has been a detriment to the organization and the fans.

I asked friends what they would choose in a fantasy question. The Lions shocking the football world and winning the Super Bowl this year, or this book selling 10,000 copies? We all chose the latter. This is a surprise for me since one of my dreams and tops on my bucket list was watching my grid iron heroes win the big game. But the reality of my life won out.

A survey came out recently about the most loyal fans in the NFL. Amazingly, Lions fans were ranked 28th out of 32 cities. When looking into the survey, it became clear that the rankings were based most likely on ticket prices. The Lions moved up from 23rd highest cost of a ticket to 5th this year with an average price of $391. This high cost includes the club level seating, which is very expensive.

The top three teams for fan loyalty were Dallas, New England, and the New York Jets. The sports radio shows were shocked that Green Bay and Washington were ranked 13 and 14. Those cities are widely known to have among the most avid, passionate fans in the NFL. It is much easier to be a loyal fan of a franchise that has produced consistent winning teams and championships. Although I am clearly biased being born and living in Detroit my entire life, I would put Lions fans in the top five.

So now I come to the main message of this third edition of the book. I am stunned at the ongoing commitment, passion, and loyalty of the Detroit Lions fan base. How do fans who have been disappointed and frustrated year after year, decade after decade, continue to love this team, sell out Ford Field on a regular basis, and be so forgiving of failure?

It must represent the intense grab the NFL has over its fans. This country has gone mad for professional football and has made it the national pastime. It is also a sign of human nature. People love to have renewed hope. In the Midwest, and other areas of the country, springtime offers a re-birth after a long winter. Lions fans summon their energies every fall thinking, why not this year? Sadly, this irrational emotional response ignores the realities of the past 56 years of this organization.

It also represents the positive nature of people. To survive a difficult adult life, one must think positively and believe things can turn around. Our country's history has shown how we come back after failure. The citizens of Detroit are experiencing another test of their strength, as every fall there is new hope."

The Lions beat the New England Patriots 40-9 in their third exhibition game this year. They looked very good in a solid effort, especially since Calvin Johnson did not play. However, we all know the preseason means nothing. We will not get a good feel for this year's team until after the first four games of the regular season. The biggest negative from the game was the continued problem with personal fouls—Lions players losing their tempers after the play. We have had 10 personal fouls in the first three exhibition games. During the season, that can cost you a game. A theory on sports radio is that Schwartz quietly supports the out-of-control behavior because it makes the team what it is, even though we are not yet sure what that is.

As I bring the new chapter to a close, it is time to offer my professional advice as a clinical social worker. Do you know a loved one who is a Lions addict? Does this loved one believe in the team year after year, decade after decade, no matter how many times they lose? Do they show severe mood swings during and after the games? Are they depressed from Sunday at 4 p.m. until Tuesday at 9 a.m. most weeks in the fall? Have they damaged things in the family room because they begin to throw things at the television in the fourth quarter when yet another game has slipped away? When their spouse tells them it's either me or the Lions—do they pick the Lions?

Don't worry! There is help available for your friends and family members. In a unique offer, I have decided to begin Lions support groups at my private practice in Ann Arbor, Michigan. During these support groups, fans will learn how to work the "10 steps" to recovery from their Lions addiction:

Step 1: Repeat the mantra, "the Lions will never go to the Super Bowl" daily.

Step 2: Call your sponsor if you begin to believe the Lions will win a playoff game this year.

Step 3: Accept that you have no control over your Lions addiction and ask a higher power to guide you through the darkness.

Step 4: Accept that the curse of Bobby Layne is real and may last for 100 years.

Step 5: If the Lions are in a close game entering the fourth quarter, turn off your television, hug your wife or husband, or play with your dog. Do not turn the television back on.

Step 6: When fantasies of winning enter your mind, remember the Lions' one playoff win since 1957.

Step 7: If we have another losing season, tell yourself, "I am not a loser, I am not a loser," over and over.

Step 8: Understand that fans in other cities are hurting also; maybe not as much as us, but they are hurting.

Step 9: Take care of yourself physically. If you live to be 100, you may see another playoff win.

Step 10: Attend your support group weekly during the fall. If you experience prolonged periods of rage, depression, or hope for the season, call our 24-hour hotline at 1-800-GET-A-LIFE.

For information on Lions fan support groups, call my office at 734-444-4839.

The final exhibition game has arrived. These games are so boring that I'm not sure I will watch more than the first quarter. There are rumors that the Lions are trying to find another receiver. That means that Ryan Broyles is not where he should be after his second knee operation in the past two years or that the bruised knee Calvin Johnson has is more than a bruise. As is usual, Schwartz is not talking. It was reported that our number one draft choice, Ziggy Ansah, sustained a concussion this week in practice. We have no idea if it will keep him out of the season opener on September 8th.

If Ziggy does not play in the first game, it will be the third straight year that our first-round draft choice did not play in the opening game of the season. Fairley was out with a foot injury two years ago, Riley Reiff was not ready to start last year, and now Ziggy appears doubtful against the Vikings. Is this just coincidence or possibly more proof of a Lions curse?

The Lions beat the Buffalo Bills 35-13 in the final exhibition game. They ended up 3-1 for the preseason, which means nothing. So now we wait the next nine days until the opener. Schwartz has to get the roster down to 53 by August 31st. One of the reasons that this is an exciting time is that you never know which way the team is going to go. The fact that Schwartz has had three out of four losing seasons puts the odds in favor of a losing season looming. As a fan who has been so disappointed and angry over the years, I have mixed feelings. The kid in me wants them to win 11 games. The adult in me, who has been tortured over time, is more realistic and believes it will be a difficult season. I have predicted the Lions will be no better than 7-9 this year.

I heard a few interesting things about the Lions recently. First, a study showed that fans of losing NFL teams eat 16 percent more saturated fats during and after games to cope with their disappointment, leading to weight gain. Fans of winning NFL teams eat nine percent fewer saturated fats and healthier foods than losing fans. No wonder we have so many fat people walking around Detroit!

The second interesting media report was about our quarterback Matt Stafford. His record against teams with winning records is 1-23. That is amazing! I told my buddy that this must be a mistake. He told me it was no mistake—it was reported by a solid reporter from ESPN. This statistic supports those who have called for Shaun Hill to be the starter. I know they pay Stafford a lot of money, but I thought the idea was to play the guy who gives the team the best chance of winning.

I am asking myself, why I have told people that Stafford is the best QB in a Lions uniform that I have seen in my lifetime? We have had very few great QBs in my lifetime, the last one being Bobby Layne in the 1950s. I liked Greg Landry (the last Lion QB to be selected to the Pro Bowl in the 1970s) and Gary Denielson. I was swept away by Stafford's strong arm; his 5,000-yard season two years ago; and the chemistry between him and Calvin Johnson, who is clearly the best receiver in the League. It is also because of the great come-from-behind wins two years ago late in the games. I have great respect for Stafford's leadership and the toughness he displayed in his rookie season, winning the game on the last play against Cleveland with a separated shoulder.

But maybe Stafford is not as good as we think; 1-23 against teams with winning records is a serious problem. This is without question a very important year for Stafford, Schwartz, and Martin Mayhew.

The Lions lost the last eight games of the season last year. In 2010, they won their last four games (which won me $250 from a bet) and then the first five games in 2011. They had a nine-game winning streak for the first time since 1953-1954. They lost seven of their last eight games in 2007 before losing all 16 games in 2008. Even the Lions will never lose 23 out of 24 again.

So why would fans be so hopeful this year when the team has lost eight in a row? That is how strong of a hold the Lions addiction/illness has on fans.

A friend of mine joked with me recently that Lions fans should file a class action lawsuit against the team for pain and suffering! That would be pretty funny. I'm not sure a judge would see it that way, however.

I had an idea several years ago to get a million Lions fans to each pay $1,000 and buy the team from William Clay Ford for $1 billion. We could then elect our own board and CEO, who would hire a new president, GM, and head coach. Okay, that's not likely to happen, but you have to be good at dreaming and fantasy to survive as a Lions fan.

I was having lunch in Dearborn recently at Matti's Deli, and the owner, Lou, said something pretty funny. I told him about the upcoming third edition of this book, and he said, "I hate those guys." He said a service came in once to buy food for the players and he told him he wasn't interested in providing lunch for the Lions! A few years ago, he had a promotion for 20 percent off lunch if you brought in a ticket to a Lions game in which they lost. Of course, the past 10 years fans have had plenty of losing tickets. He had *The Detroit News* write an article about the promotion, so it was a profitable venture. As I was walking out, he wanted me to hear it one more time: "I hate those guys."

One of my students from Eastern Michigan University, Craig, told me that he hates the Lions, too. When I asked why, he told me that as a kid, he would visit his family often and the Lions game was always on the TV. He wanted to watch cartoons, so he always resented the Lions. As an adult, he became a Dallas Cowboys fan. Not a bad team to adopt. The Lions once again disappoint a young fan.

It is September 5th, 2013. Opening day in the NFL with the Broncos hosting the world champion Ravens. Our Lions begin in three days. Vegas has come out with their odds for a team winning the Super Bowl. The Lions are 40:1 odds to win the big game. They are in the middle of the pack, but are ahead of two teams that made the playoffs last year, the Colts and Vikings. The teams favored to win the Super Bowl are Denver and San Francisco at 6:1 odds.

Twelve distinguished ESPN football analysts and reporters made their predictions for the upcoming NFL season. All 12 had the Packers winning the NFC North, with several of them picking the Packers to win the Super Bowl. None picked Detroit to win their division, but one said they would make the playoffs as a wild card team. Most-picked was Denver, San Francisco, or Seattle to win the Super Bowl. Several picked Ziggy Ansah to win the defensive rookie of the year. The good news for Lions fans is that Ziggy participated in the full practice today for the first time in 12 days. He may be able to play in the opener Sunday.

The founder of the website Pro Football Talk in West Virginia made the strangest prediction for the NFL I have ever heard. He predicts that our Lions—yes, our beloved Lions—will go to the playoffs this year. They will win the first playoff game at Washington, then go on to beat the 49'ers on the road before losing at Green Bay to the Packers in the NFC championship game. Is he out of his mind? He wants us to believe that a team that has won one playoff game the past 55 years and went 4-12 last year will win two playoff games this year? If he really believes this, his credibility is in danger. He may have said it as a publicity stunt. I can tell you with great confidence that the Lions will not win two playoff games this year. I would be willing to make a $10,000 bet, as Mitt Romney would say.

As the 2013 season begins with Peyton Manning throwing for seven TDs and over 450 yards in the opener against the Ravens, it is time for my one and only prediction for the Lions as the book goes to print this week. They are favored by five points over the Vikings, but I see us losing 27-17. I hope I am wrong—most of my friends are predicting a Lions win. I see this opening game as a must-win for Detroit. If they lose, they face the possibility of going 0-3 with two difficult road games to follow at Arizona and Washington. If they win, they would have an outside shot at going 3-1 after the first four games.

Now I'm worried—really worried—about the Lions fans. Two days before the opening game, fans are calling in to the radio shows with their predictions for the season. The Lions addiction/illness is getting stronger. Two fans said 10-6, one said 11-5, and another said 14-2! The reasons given included that Tony Scheffler is going to have a breakout year. Another one was that Ziggy Ansah is going to have a big year. Fans do not understand what it takes to win. Offensive line play, defense, coaching, and great ownership. Fantasy football has shifted much of the fan focus towards the skill positions. Another fan called in and said that he just bet his friend a month's salary ($800) that the Lions would beat the Packers on Thanksgiving Day this year. The illness is strongest just before opening day; I should not be surprised.

It is September 7th, 2013, the day before we open the season against the Vikings at Ford Field. Most are picking the Lions to win this one; they are 5¼ point favorites. I will watch the game with some friends tomorrow. I now watch a little bit less as a die-hard fan and more as an objective observer with the task of finishing this book. It will be interesting to see if the passionate fan in me comes out.

Suh was voted as one of the six captains for the Lions this year—the first time he was voted by the team. He was quoted in the *Detroit Free Press* telling his team that, "The Super Bowl is well within reach." I understand a team captain trying to motivate the players, but really? The Super Bowl is within reach if they get tickets from the NFL or buy them on Stub Hub!

September 8th, 2013: It's finally here! The opener against the Vikings that fans have been waiting for the past eight months. It's a cloudy late summer day in Detroit with a threat of rain. If the Lions lose, the weather is right for a mood of depression for Lions fans. If we win, it will feel like the sun is out. The pregame show reports that *Sports Illustrated* rates the Lions number 15 out of 16 teams in the NFC. Wow! Experts can have very different opinions, but that is not good.

The president of the Lions, Tom Lewand, is interviewed on the pregame show and said that the major message from fans has been that the 10-6 season in 2011 was more representative of this team, and last year's 4-12 record was more of the aberration. I see it as exactly the opposite: the 10-6 season was the aberration. We will know who is right in a few months.

The pregame show featured a die-hard Lions fan who was tailgating at Eastern Market. He had an RV decked out in blue and silver. His toilet has a picture of Matt Millen at the bottom of the bowl! Now that is an example of the passion fans have; we don't forget the brutal history of the team over the past 56 years.

The sun comes out a half hour before the season kicks off. The sun always improves one's mood and sense of hope. I was not sure I would feel it as the opener approached, but the fan in me has emerged. I want to win and have a successful season no matter how it affects the sales of my book. I like Jim Schwartz and don't want to see him lose his job.

As kick off approaches, my last thought is, "God help our Detroit Lions and their fans."

We look great on the first drive. We have 2nd down and a foot and miss on two straight plays. And then our first "I Don't Believe It!" moment of the season. Botched snap, missed field goal. And on the first offensive play for the Vikings, Adrian Peterson runs up the middle 78 yards for a touchdown. You can't make this stuff up!

The Lions fight back and get an apparent TD with an amazing catch by Calvin. But guess what? It looks like he did not complete the "process of the catch." Where have we heard that before? Chicago, 2010!

The boos began within 10 minutes of the first quarter. I'm not surprised. Here is where reality hits Lions fans. The preseason is over. On the fourth and 1 at the 15, Schwartz gambles and goes for it; Joique Bell runs for the first down. But Brandon Pettigrew is flagged for holding! Detroit settles for a field goal.

Oh, my God! Suh is called for a chop block on an interception return by DeAndre Levy for a TD. He wasn't even in the play. So much for not making silly plays. It is the second lost touchdown by the Lions in the first half. And then, on the first play Stafford throws an interception! I don't believe it.

With nine minutes to go, our corner Bill Bentley jumps a route and drops the interception that would have gone for a

TD. Those are the plays that change games and winning teams make. The stats show the Lions have dropped five passes in the first half, then on the next play, Pettigrew fumbles after getting a first down. Louis Delmas then shows the Vikings how tough he is and bumps helmets after a play for a 15-yard personal foul. Another false start! Bell leaps over the line and the ball comes out! It is being reviewed. Touchdown! Is the Lions' luck changing? The second half will tell.

The crowd is quiet as the Lions are about to take the lead. Another TD lost when Calvin catches an apparent TD, but his second foot comes down on the line—no TD! I think fans are afraid to get too excited; they should be very loud to help their team. The first half has shaken the fans' confidence. Are we going to be heartbroken again? Best to be cautious. Bush runs it in for a TD. Lions get their first lead 20-14. But no, another TD that does not count, his knee hit the ground. Bell finishes it off though to take the lead.

When I asked my family and friends gathered for the big game today who will win, my wife, Zoe, said the Lions will lose because they likely have some more big mistakes in them. She understands the Lions well. Wow, Bush runs a short pass in from 77 yards! Lions 27-17.

Last year, the Lions allowed 158 points in fourth quarter—the third most in the NFL. The Vikings fumble it back to Detroit with 11 minutes left in the game. Will the Lions put them away? My friend Bart falls asleep while watching, clearly not a die-hard fan. A roughing the passer by the Vikings keeps the ball for the Lions. Hey, wait, that's our play! A pass interference penalty by the Vikings keeps the drive alive. Bush for a TD—wait, his knee hit at the one-yard line. TD to the tight end! The Lions are up ten, 34-24.

I am exhausted watching this game. So many ups and downs. The Lions are showing me something today; they are fighting back impressively and getting past their mistakes. My friend said that this chapter was writing itself when it looked bad.

A great special teams play downing a punt at the one-yard line. Give the Lions credit; they have played a great second half. I might have to scrap this book project. Oh, I forgot, there are 15 games left! Should I go with the title that I was hoping for: *I Don't Believe It – We're Good?* Final score of the opener Lions 34-24. Suh is fined $100,000 for his illegal hit—the biggest fine ever given by the NFL. Once again there is a major distraction instead of focusing on football. The Lions have led the NFL in personal fouls since 2009 with 116. The Eagles are second with 101. Does that make the Lions tough or stupid? I will go with the latter.

So, Lions fans, another season is under way. Are you ready for the rollercoaster ride? Be strong, control your emotions, and get help if you need it. Who knows what the title of my fourth edition of this book will be sometime around 2020.

Several things have become clear to me after this opening game. First, I owe an apology to the Fords, Martin Mayhew, and Jim Schwartz. It is obvious that the past 56 years of losing was just bad luck, and the Lions jinx is now over. It may have ended at half time today as Coach Schwartz addressed the team. I am ashamed and embarrassed that I doubted the team and the organization the way I have. The only thing to be determined is, will the Lions go undefeated this year on the way to the Super Bowl?

CHAPTER 4

I Still Don't Believe It:
Update to the 2nd Edition

WHAT ELSE COULD POSSIBLY GO WRONG FOR THE LIONS since I ended the first edition of this book in May of 2006? Perhaps a coach who was driving naked through a Wendy's late-night window; a player being suspended for drug use and then being accused of inappropriate sexual conduct at a local strip bar while carrying a gun a year later; or the sighting of a "Fire Millen" sign at a Colorado/New York baseball game at the start of summer? Was it the trip to Oakland last year in one day to test how tough the team was—they weren't! Maybe it was the vote about the Lions' president being the most ineffective executive in all four major sports? How about cutting the NFL's #2 overall pick last year after cutting the NFL's #3 overall pick the year before?

Fans, we are proud to celebrate the 50th anniversary of the Lions last championship this year. After several years of anger, disloyalty, and rooting for the other team, I have decided to return as a Lions fan. My recovery from the depression, rage, and hopelessness is complete. I did follow through on not renewing my season tickets, however. I missed being a fan of the team. I am genuinely excited about seeing Calvin Johnson this year—the man they are calling the next Jerry Rice of the NFL. Even the Lions can't screw him up, can they? There is a buzz about the team around the NFL. Many people believe they could be much improved in Marinelli's second year as head coach. The only thing working against a nine-win season is their past 50-year history and a very tough schedule this season.

The 2006 season was filled with "I Don't Believe It!" moments. There were the 63 sacks of Jon Kitna, which led the NFL. I have to give him credit; he is one tough football player. I was at the San Francisco game last season when he was blindsided by a linebacker on a blitz. This guy hit Kitna so hard that he was propelled three feet into the air before coming down on his back and snapping his helmet to the turf. I thought the guy had killed him! I could not believe that Kitna got up and stayed in the game. No one can ever question this guy's toughness or character.

How about the predictions from Roy Williams that the team would win their last 10 games of 2006? Williams has also recently predicted that the Lions would be able to score 50 points a game! Kitna predicted the team would go 11-5 in 2007. Maybe the guys shouldn't make predictions; they don't seem to be very good at it.

It is July 7th, 2007 as I update this book that sold 1,200 copies in its first NFL season in print. I had a great time on some of the sports radio shows that were nice enough to give me airtime to promote the book and talk about the Lions. I want to thank Mark Wilson and Rob Parker of WCHB 1200 AM, who had me on several times last year. Thank you to Sean Baligian of WDFN 1130 of the FAN, who gave me my first radio exposure in September of 2006. It was great meeting so many fans at book signings at Borders stores. Thanks to Sam Speigel and Mick Dolinski of Partners Distribution, Inc. for getting the book on the shelves at Borders. Thank you also to Alex Kellogg of the *Detroit Free Press* for writing a great article about the book in the fall of 2006. Also, thanks to Tom from 336 Main Street in Plymouth who hosted by first book signing, and to the Book Cellar in Plymouth for being the first store to put *I Don't Believe It* on the shelves. People love to talk about the Lions and the NFL.

The Lions continue to be the butt of many jokes on a national level. Jay Mariotti from Chicago recently said on an ESPN show that Matt Millen should resign and end the humiliation to himself and the Detroit Lions organization. After a "Fire Millen" sign was displayed during a June baseball game in Colorado that has nothing to do with a Detroit team, he felt it was time for a change. Mr. Ford does not agree.

On the next ESPN national show, *Pardon the Interruption*, the hosts described a ceremony in Florida for Lions head coach Rod Marinelli, at which the high school football stadium where he played was named after him. During the ceremony, one of Marinelli's sons told the story of how his father once wrestled a bear in high school. He beat the bear! The two hosts of the show said that Marinelli should bring a bear to training camp this year and show his linemen how to "get low" on the bear. The hosts said getting low was the key to being victorious in a battle.

They were clearly making fun of the Lions' organization, Millen and Marinelli. It is embarrassing as a fan of the team to see media constantly making fun of your team and your city.

I would love to see the team turn around this year and bring some pride back to a once-proud franchise.

There has been talk on some national sports shows that this is Millen's last chance. Bill Cowher, who left the Steelers, is supposedly interested in getting back into the game after the 2007 season. He will only take a position where he has total control as the general manager, as well as the head coaching position. The Lions would have to be crazy not to give him the position, especially if the 2007 season is another disaster.

As fans, it seems that all we ask at this point is an exciting brand of football, improvement from the previous year, and hope for the future. After having a 3-13 season in 2006, a 7-9 record would probably keep fans from another uprising. The Lions need to score more touchdowns, especially from the red zone. They need to pull out some victories in the last few minutes instead of falling short. They also need to have some "game breaking" plays to get the fans excited. Dre Bly had many interceptions a few years ago, which really got the crowd going. We haven't had that kind of excitement since the great days of Barry Sanders. You loved watching games with Sanders whether the Lions won or lost.

As the summer winds down to the fall in September and the nights grow cooler, sports fans turn their anticipation to the NFL season. You really can't tell that much about a team during the four preseason games that are rather boring to watch. There is nothing quite like looking forward to the first regular season game in early September. Hope is always high; maybe this will be the year we turn it around. Detroit opens on the road against the Raiders this season. They were the only team with a worse record than the Lions last year. So, we will watch the worst two teams from the 2006 NFL season start the 2007 season. The game will showcase the two top draft picks from this year in Jemarcus Russell and Calvin Johnson. It should be interesting.

ESPN had a national poll of sports fans about which professional team was the worst. The Chicago Cubs edged out the Lions 38 percent to 34 percent. The LA Clippers came in third. One of our local sports stations then asked listeners to call and give their opinions. One guy calls and says, "You have to be kidding me—it's the Lions hands down, and I'll tell you why. Barry Sanders actually 'paid not to play!' He actually paid back his six million dollars in salary not to play for the Lions. Most athletes don't like to return six million dollars instead of finishing their contract with an organization." I thought this was hilarious.

Other Lions news included that charges would not be filed against Shaun Rogers for his incident in a strip club recently. This is good news for Detroit's defense, as he can now line up next to the highest paid defensive lineman in the NFL, Cory Redding. The Lions signed him to a seven-year, $49 million contract, with $30 million guaranteed! Mike and Mike on the national ESPN radio show were making fun of the Lions for giving that much money to a player who was unproven based on one or two good seasons. The Lions are always getting national attention—mostly the wrong kind! Another national sports show was saying how the Lions are the most improved team in the League this year and will go 10-6. When someone from Detroit called in and asked them to go down their schedule and find 10 wins, the guy backtracked and said it looks more like seven or eight wins. Training camp opens in one week—this is getting exciting!

Calvin Johnson finally signed today, August 3rd, 2007. I can't wait to see him play this week. I think he received $27 million guaranteed. The bad news is that our second pick in the draft, Drew Stanton from Michigan State, hurt his knee and is out for the year. Millen said early in the week that his knee was structurally sound and that he "just tweaked it." It turned out to be more than a "tweak." Many people questioned using the second pick for a back-up quarterback that would not help the team for at least two years. We could have had the great linebacker out of Michigan or the top linebacker in the draft out of Penn State. We definitely need help on the defense. Teddy Lehman is injured again and is not expected to play for a few weeks. It seems he has been hurt his entire career with Detroit.

A friend of mine recently told me a story about the Lions that may shed some light onto why the organization seems to struggle year after year after year. His friend called the Lions ticket office this summer asking about tickets for the Thanksgiving Day game against the Packers. It was his father's 80th birthday and he wanted 20 tickets for the family to celebrate. The Lions told him that he could get 20 tickets, but not together. They said they would be in groups of four in different sections. He was disappointed with this news. They then told him that he could get the seats all together, but only if he bought 50 tickets! He was not happy when he heard this. Is this any way to treat fans after we have remained loyal through this nightmare? Besides terrible football, the Lions offer us poor public relations.

At the end of July 2007, our leader William Clay Ford gave a rare interview about the Lions. He said that he had complete faith in the job Matt Millen was doing with the team and felt he had done an excellent job as team president. Are you kidding me? The radio talk shows had a field day with this. Has Mr. Ford seen what is going on here the last six years? I said in the first edition of this book that Mr. Ford loves Millen like a son and nothing is going to change that. His endorsement of Millen in the way that he did it, is all you need to know about the problems of this organization. I am guessing that 90 percent of the NFL teams would have fired their presidents after the results of the last six seasons.

I wanted to interview Marc Spindler for the update of this book, but I couldn't figure out how to reach him. I met him at one of the WXYT sports shows last year. He was kind enough to sit down with me for 10 minutes and talk Lions football. He told me he couldn't believe I didn't interview him for the book because he had a lot of great Lions stories. One of the stories he told me is that he was responsible for ending Scott Mitchell's career with the Lions. In a game against the Bengals, Spindler blocked a field goal that sent the game into overtime. Mitchell ended up throwing an interception that was returned for a touchdown, ending the game. Mitchell's career came to an end with Detroit shortly after this. I could not believe how big Spindler was—the NFL players look like they come from another planet! The phone number I got was the wrong number, and even though I heard he lived in Clarkston, I could not get in touch with him. If you see the book, Marc, contact me and we will do the interview for the next update. I will call it "conversations with a Lion."

So, fans, get ready for the 2007 season of Detroit Lions football. Will it be another major disappointment or will we be surprised by a solid performance and improvement? Will we need to begin a Lions fan support group to get through the emotions? Will we feel the anger, frustration, and heartbreak that we know so well? For those who have done the hard work of recovering from the addiction, stay strong. Stay away if you have to, but don't relapse into the Lions illness we talked about in the first edition. Keep the faith, keep hope alive. Go Lions?

CHAPTER 5

Two Moments in Lions History Never Forgotten

IN NOVEMBER OF 1970, MY BEST FRIEND WOODY AND I were watching what would become one of the most memorable moments in Detroit Lions history. I was 15 and Woody was 16. Being sports nuts, we followed the four major sport teams in Detroit with an amazing passion. But our devotion to NFL football and to our Lions was unique. The average fan may find it is a complicated and difficult game to understand, because what appears to be obvious is not. It is a thinking man's game, much like a chess match. I have often compared it to war, led by generals, with a football flying instead of bullets. Of the four major sports, football fields the most players, 22, at the same time. Baseball, 10 to 13, basketball 10, hockey 12. Due to how difficult this sport is, and how crucial strategy becomes, the head coach in football is more important than in any other major sport. I believe this is what makes football so special, and why fans' passions are so intense.

Let's get back to that day in 1970. We were at Woody's house in Detroit watching what should be the first of many more "I

Don't Believe It!" moments concerning our beloved Detroit
Lions. The Lions were leading New Orleans 17-16 with a few seconds left on the clock. Tom Dempsey was about to make history,
kicking a 63-yard field goal to beat Detroit, ripping our hearts
out for the first of many times to come. Attempting a field goal
from that distance seemed almost laughable. In fact, it was said
that lineman Alex Karris was laughing so hard that he never got
set in his position for the kick. Watching that kick, I remember
hearing the thud of the kicker's foot (Dempsey was disabled,
being born with a deformed foot) striking the ball and watching
it fall incredibly just over the uprights. The Saints won. Woody
and I looked at each other and at the same time screamed, "I
don't believe it!"

Flash forward to December 19th, 2004, the Lions vs. the
Vikings. That was the game that finally inspired me to write this
book. Once again, the expression "I don't believe it" proved appropriate. In the last minute of the fourth quarter, Joey Harrington
led the Lions down the field to score the apparent tying
touchdown that would send the game into overtime. Winning
this game was crucial because, after starting the season 4-2,
Harrington and the team had suffered a terrible stretch, losing
seven of their last eight games. More importantly, they still had
a very good chance of making the playoffs (due to how many
teams in the NFC were struggling). When they came on the field
for the extra point, they seemed to be taking an especially long
time with the kick. The holder kept looking back at the kicker
to make sure he was ready. At that moment, something strange
happened. Maybe because of my 34 years of experience as a fan,
I thought to myself, "They are going to miss the extra point."
Botched snap, game over. "I don't believe it." One of the radio

announcers for Minnesota said, "The Lions don't believe they can win." Harrington's lips read, "Unbelievable."

The year 2004 was a particularly strange one for me as a Lions fan. It was the year I finally snapped. I was excited about their 4-2 start; I was sure they would go to the playoffs, and the rebuilding program under Millen was beginning to work. We had drafted and developed some great young talent. We felt we had the coach to lead the team into the future. In 2006, the Super Bowl was going to be in Detroit; maybe our Lions would be playing in front of their home crowd! Back to reality.

CHAPTER 6

Memories of Detroit Sports as a Teenager

WOODY IS A RADIO ENGINEER. I REMEMBER US BEING down in his basement as teenagers, and how he was always fooling around with ham radios. After we didn't see each other for about 15 years, I saw him on TV doing the NBA finals with Michael Jordan. He had headphones on and was the radio engineer for the NBA. I had no idea he had become that successful from his hobby as a teenager. He works the World Series, Super Bowl, and college football and basketball championships. He invited me to the national championship game for college football in Miami a few years ago.

An article in the national sports magazine, *Sports Business Journal*, said Woody has seen more champion-ship games than Michael Jordan and Derrick Jeter added together. I am proud of Woody for what he has achieved in life. We have become great friends again these past 10 years. We remain passionate about sports, but mostly we are great golf buddies.

Woody and I were best friends as teenagers. We met when I was 12 years old. There is something unique about a childhood friendship. It stays with you the rest of your life. Woody and I would spend hours together centered on sports. I slept over at his house quite often on weekends. During the winter, we would make an ice rink in his backyard. We would wake up at 3:00 a.m. to give it another coat of water. We both loved hockey and grew up watching Gordie Howe at the end of his career. We built a makeshift hockey net one year out of two-by-fours and an old blanket. We would get dressed in all the goalie gear that Woody's brother had; when we shot the puck, it would hit the wooden post and the net would collapse. Those are great memories.

When we went to Olympia Stadium to see Gordie Howe, Alex Delvecchio, Frank Mahovlich, and Mickey Redmond, we found a unique way to get into the stadium. We went to almost every home game for a few years, but the ticket price of $7 was hard to afford. One night, we were looking for tickets outside the stadium, and a guy with a *Columbo* trench coat calls us over. He says, "You guys want to get into the game for $2? Just go through that gate with that usher and say, 'Hi, Louie.'" We paid our $2, and there'd be a different password every night. We did this for a year or two, before their operation got busted and we had to buy tickets the old-fashioned way. We will never forget our days down at Olympia.

Woody and I went to a Tigers game one night and parked far from the stadium to save money. When we came back to the car after the game, we noticed a gang of five or six suspicious-looking teens following us. We could sense they were about to jump us so we made a run for the car. I had my arm in a sling due to separation and ran the best I could. We just got to the car and got in when these kids reached us, and began pulling on the doors just as we locked them. Woody began beeping the horn, which got them to run. Our hearts were in our throats. We were very lucky that night.

My father died when I was six years old and my mother had significant problems afterward. My teenage years were filled with stress and uncertainty. My attachment to friends and sports was an effort to fill the void I felt in my life. Something always seemed to be missing for me. The passion I got from playing and following sports was important to me. It was a great escape. Sports represents a great escape for many people, for many different reasons.

All people, I have found, have different experiences growing up in their families. Some have typical, happy childhoods, raised by fairly normal parents. Many are not as lucky and grow up around multiple stresses and problems. I was actually quite lucky in some ways because I had older siblings who lessened some of the problems our family faced after our father's death in 1962. As a social worker, I have seen many sad things happen to people and families over my 25 years of practice. Death, divorce, alcoholism, child abuse, suicide, medical and mental illness, and depression can hit any family. Everyone learns to cope and go on through life the best way they can. We learn our coping strengths from our parents and families. Some people learn to cope with anything life throws their way and are well-adjusted, happy people. Others never recover from early trauma and problems and go through life angry, depressed, or unhappy.

I have been very lucky in my life. I have learned to cope as a process of facing bad decisions and disasters. I have never had much money, but I do all right. I have survived two divorces and feel I understand myself and relationships better now. I am the best father I know how to be to my son and daughter, and I have a wonderful wife who helps me grow as a person. Sports is simply one of the distractions in my life; I take the winning and losing less seriously than I used to, but winning is definitely better. Everyone needs a hobby!

Sports offer a wonderful escape from the pressure of life. Watching or participating are both healthy ways to take a break from life. Golf is the sport I play. As many people know, this can be a rather frustrating endeavor and may not be considered relaxing by many. I have gotten pretty good at the game by learning patience and never giving up. I am a 10 handicap and got my first hole in one in 2007. I also enjoy shooting a basketball, although I am not very good at the game because of a bad leg. I have a pretty good shot, however, and can beat people at horse, three-point shooting, or best out of 20 foul shots.

CHAPTER 7

Is There a Lions Curse?

IN 2004, THE LIONS FANS SEEM TO HAVE FINALLY LOST IT. I have never seen so much anger and frustration by fans. Some people make it too important; it is just a game, after all, isn't it? I am worried that fans are about to take things too far as the 2004 season comes to an end. Some fans are a little "disturbed," if you know what I mean. They have terrible tempers. The most dangerous crowd I have ever been in was when I went to see Michigan play Ohio State in Columbus. The fans at the Horseshoe that day were frightening. I thought my life was at risk. Too many people were drunk; too many people were acting like their lives were coming to an end as Ohio State lost that day. I hope that never happens with the Lions at Ford Field.

Woody asked me if I wanted to join him in Jacksonville for a November 2004 Lions game. We went down and golfed twice before the Sunday game; we got to play the famous 17th hole at the TPC of Sawgrass; the island green par three for the Players Championship. What a great experience. Saturday night, I helped Woody set up his radio booth for the game. I had the opportunity to go into the Lions locker room as the crew was unloading their equipment. I saw their helmets, pads, and shoes lined up in the lockers. Again, it reminded me of soldiers preparing to go to war. After almost 35 years as a fan, here I was in my Lions' locker room on the road. It hit me just how much this team meant to me. The pride I felt of being from Detroit.

People in the United States are all pretty much the same. For the most part, they are friendly and care about their families, work hard, and live by the rules. People have pride in the cities they grew up in and live in as adults. The only cities that are a little different are New York and Los Angeles—they are different because of their size, but even in those cities, there are great people who are very proud of where they live. There is something that gives people a special feeling when the team from their city wins a championship. It's as though the fan feels like he or she is a winner. They feel that they are special for at least those few weeks.

Game day saw clouds and 40-mile-an-hour winds (I was hoping for some Florida sunshine). The Lions were losing 17-0 when I had to leave at the end of the third quarter to catch my plane home. I heard Eddie Drummond's first punt return for a touchdown in the car; when I got to the airport and saw a television, I was amazed to see a 17-17 tie in overtime. Drummond had run another back all the way in the last minute to tie the game. We lost in overtime; the offense never touched the ball.

I have been a season ticket holder in three stadiums over the years. I have seen games in Tiger Stadium, the Silverdome, and now Ford Field. I will recall some of the great times through this book. It has not all been torture, just most of it. As I said, 2004 had been a particularly hard one for me. I was having problems waiting for a great team. There have been times I have told friends that the Lions look like they are playing a different sport than the best teams in the NFL. The games just look different.

I "snapped" again after we blew a 19-7 lead at Minnesota in December 2004. Adjustments by the coach at halftime are critical in football; we had not done well in this area this season. I knew I was in a bad state of mind when I was openly rooting for the Arizona Cardinals to beat the Lions. I had never done that in 34 years of following the team. I was actually disappointed when the Lions won the game—their only win in eight games. I knew the pressure of being a Lions fan was finally starting to get to me. I would often joke with friends that being a Lions fan was not good for one's mental health. Being a social worker, I felt that there should be an official psychiatric disorder in the DSM-IV referring to the risks and symptoms of following this team for any extended period of time. I had become bitter and angry. I felt I had to disconnect emotionally from this team that I loved. Sometimes you just need to walk away from a relationship that is bringing you down. I will miss my team, but hope to be back in the future—I know I will never stop loving them.

I feel so bad for Mr. Ford and his family who have owned the team since 1964. I'm sure no one wants to bring a Super Bowl title to Detroit more than he does. I hear he is a fantastic person. I am convinced that this city would celebrate a Super Bowl championship more intensely than any other for the Tigers, Red Wings, or Pistons. The city would go crazy! It's hard to know what the answer is, but a lot of people with a lot of experience are working on it. I hope they get it right. Before I die, I want to watch my Lions win a Super Bowl. Okay, maybe just play in a Super Bowl.

The Lions won three championships from 1935-1957 and were 6-1 in playoff games. Since 1957, they are 1-9 in playoff games; the only win that I witnessed was the 38-6 victory over Dallas in 1991. That was the year we appeared in the NFC championship game. Is that the closest we will ever be to the Super Bowl? I hope not.

Before we review the highlights and lowlights since 1970, I want to address the so-called Honolulu blue and silver curse. Does it really exist? Has this organization had far more bad luck than any other professional sports team in history? I think the answer might be yes! Besides finding amazing ways to lose games, the Lions have had an unbelievable amount of personal tragedy on and off the field. I was in the crowd at Tiger Stadium that horrible day October 24th, 1971, two days before my 16th birthday. Chuck Hughes died that day of a heart attack after running a pass route. I remember Dick Butkus signaling to the sidelines that something was seriously wrong with Chuck. I remember getting home from the game, won by the Bears, and finding out that Hughes had died. Not many sports fans can say they saw a player die during a game.

I came very close to seeing my second Detroit Lions player die on December 21st, 1997. It happened when I went to the Jets game. The Lions needed to win to make the playoffs, and Barry Sanders was closing in on 2000 yards rushing. The Lions' outstanding linebacker, Reggie Brown, did not move after a collision involving his neck. You could tell it was very serious. I thought back to the game with Chuck Hughes. Was I really witnessing the death of a second Lions player 26 years later? We were very worried about that possibility and were amazed at hearing how close he came to death that day. The work of the trainer and the doctor saved his life.

Other tragedies include the death of Coach Don McCafferty during training camp in 1974. Eric Andolsek's death in a bizarre accident during the off-season. Mike Utley's being paralyzed during a game. I'm not sure if any other professional team has ever had to deal with more tragedy. Is there a jinx? Why does such a black cloud seem to hang over this organization? Only time will tell.

The Internet provides a funny piece called "The Curse of Bobby Layne" (www.curseofbobbylayne.com). The website talks about the 1958 trading card for Layne. When Layne was traded to the Steelers, his trading card had him in a Lions' blue jersey. Was the mistake because he was traded so quickly, or was this an omen of things to come? The website goes on to say, "If someone or something is truly cursed, no matter what they did, no matter how hard they try, something always keeps them from succeeding. Sometimes this bending of fate leaves behind an almost humorous by-product that lingers long after the event." The website describes several Lions humiliations since Layne was traded. In 1966, Coach Harry Gilmer was pummeled by snowballs from Lions fans in Tiger Stadium. Fans started chanting "bye, bye, Harry." The Lions lost that game 28-26 and Mr. Ford fired Gilmer after the 4-9-1 record that year. He was replaced by Joe Schmidt. A fan uprising against the Lions—could it happen again?

In 1962, the Lions drafted John Hadl. They tried to convince him to switch positions and play running back. He was a quarterback in college. He thought the Lions were crazy, refused to sign with them, and ended up on the San Diego Chargers. He went on to become a six-time pro bowler. Why can't the Lions recognize talent when it's right in front of them?

Another humiliation involved draft day. Is it possible to trade your number one pick and not know it? In 1974, the Lions forgot that they traded their first-round pick, which was #13 to New Orleans with a player. The Lions attempted to make the 13th pick and were reminded that they had traded it.

In 1987, Wayne Fontes was arrested and eventually arraigned on cocaine possession and two drunk driving charges. He pleaded not guilty and was eventually promoted to head coach. After everything Mr. Ford did for Fontes, Wayne thanks him by suing the Lions in 1999, claiming his back was injured while working for the Lions and he could no longer work as a coach in the NFL. This might have been because he wasn't a very good coach! He lost the suit.

During the early 1970s, the Minnesota Vikings tortured us more than any other team. They had won 13 straight over the Lions until October 20th, 1974, when the Lions finally ended the streak with a 20-16 win. Before that, Woody and I had multiple "I don't believe it!" experiences followed by two or three days of depression all caused by our archrival Vikings. September 20th, 1971: Errol Mann misses a 33-yard field goal to tie the game as time expires. December 11th, 1971: the Lions lose to the Vikings, turning the ball over six times. The Vikings scored a touchdown in this game after the Lions blocked a field goal and the Vikings recovered the ball in the end zone for a touchdown. Even when they made a great play, it went the Vikings' way. November 12th, 1972: Bobby Bryant blocks a 33-yard field goal attempt that would have won the game for the Lions as time runs out. On November 7th, 1973, we had another Viking victory that included a blocked punt for a touchdown.

The "purple people eaters" and Fran Tarkenton tortured us

for years. How fitting it was in the December 2004 game that the Lions blow an extra point to force overtime against none other than the Minnesota Vikings. It brought back quite a few memories—all bad.

A few more horror stories from the early 1970s: On December 26th, 1970, Detroit lost 5-0 in the playoffs to the Dallas Cowboys. Greg Landry was one of the best quarterbacks of the past 40 years, and we had our all-pro corner Lem Barney on the team. Recently, I heard Barney in a radio interview say that that game bothered him so much that, to this day, some 34 years later, he did not even want to talk about it. September 29th, 1974: the Lions lost a 21-19 decision to the Green Bay Packers. Again, the Lions have a punt blocked for a safety.

In the years since their last championship, the Lions have had 34 losing seasons, 17 winning, and four .500 seasons. Their all-time record is 512-606-32. We have had one playoff victory since 1957. It seems almost impossible for one of the original franchises in the NFL.

I want to describe some of the happy times I have had being a Lions fan. Fans loved Charlie Sanders. When Woody and I were teenagers, we would throw a football across his bed and one of us would try to catch it stretched out horizontally the way Sanders did. He was the greatest Lions receiver I have ever seen. I would say Herman Moore was the second best. Charlie Sanders had one of his great days on November 26th, 1970, against the Oakland Raiders. I recall the Lions being down 14-0 at halftime and winning 28-14. Sanders made two of his classic touchdown catches; I was watching close-by near that end zone and remember what incredible catches those were. Tiger Stadium was very loud that day.

Detroit Lions football fans are amazing; they never give up. The crowds at the Silverdome were so loud, there was no question it was intimidating to visiting teams. A majority of games have been sold out at home; even at the Silverdome, with an 80,000 capacity, I bet 80 percent of the games were sold out, or near sell outs. The support for this team has been outstanding, especially considering how poorly they have performed with few results since 1957.

Our favorite Lions players since 1970 in order of athletic ability and fan appeal: Barry Sanders, Lem Barney, Charlie Sanders, Billy Sims, Herman Moore, Joe Schmidt, Alex Karras, Al "Bubba" Baker, Robert Porcher, Eddie Murray, Jason Hanson, Greg Landry, Gary Danielson, Shaun Rogers, Mel Gray, and Chris Spielman.

Barry Sanders was simply unbelievable. The greatest football player by far I have ever seen as a Lion. He was the main reason to look forward to watching the Lions for 10 years. I remember the day he retired. My buddies and I were on a five-day golfing trip in northern Michigan. We were at dinner one night after golfing 36 holes. My friend said, "I just heard that Barry Sanders announced his retirement." My friend is a practical joker, so I thought he was up to his old tricks. I bet him $20 that it was a ploy; when he thanked me for the $20 and put it in his pocket, I realized that the Lions' worst nightmare had been realized. How could Barry do it? Everyone was so looking forward to him becoming the all-time rushing leader in the next year. Lions football has never been the same since that day. A player of his caliber comes along maybe every 50 years. To this day, I will be glad to debate anyone that Barry Sanders was the greatest running back who had ever played the game.

One of my great thrills associated with the Lions was having the opportunity to meet Barry Sanders a few years after he retired. I was at a golf dome during a nasty winter night in the Detroit area. There was hardly anyone there when I came to the putting green after hitting balls. I look up and see Barry Sanders as the only other person on the green with me. I recognized him immediately and had to meet him. He was so polite and friendly; I couldn't believe it. He talked to me with no ego or star power. We mostly talked about golf; he loved the game. He met my son and daughter and gave them his autograph. I told him I met Lawrence Taylor at a golf tournament and couldn't believe how big he was. I said to Barry, "How could you survive a hit from a guy that big?" He answered, "Now you know why I ran so fast." Barry said Lawrence got him a few times, and it didn't feel very good. I offered to take Barry golfing at U of M someday since he had not played that course and wanted to. I gave him my phone number and told him I would be honored to golf with him. He thanked me and said he just might take me up on it. He never called, but what a gentleman he was to my children and me; I will never forget meeting him that day.

CHAPTER 8

On Being a Lions Fan:
Long-term Mental Health Concerns

THROUGH THE YEARS, COPIOUS AMOUNTS OF CONFUSION, bad coaching, and a general lack of confidence has destroyed many Lions teams. Making mistakes at the most crucial points of a game is a Lions trademark. These are the things that bad teams do on a regular basis and why the fans have suffered through so many seasons.

Our coach to start the 1976 season was Rick Forzano, who was fired after a 1-3 start (see Appendix A). He coached for two plus seasons and had 15 wins and 17 losses. Did you ever notice how much he patted the players on their butts? Tommy Hudspeth replaced him and went five wins, five losses the rest of the 1976 season. He coached through the 1977 season when he was 6-8. Monte Clark took over from 1978-1984. Clark's seven years as coach was the second longest stint in Lions history behind eight years for George Wilson (1957-1964), and eight years for Wayne Fontes (1989-1996). Who would have guessed that Fontes would be the most successful coach since 1957? He ended with 66 wins and 67 losses! He was our most successful coach in 49 years. This says it all.

Why can't the Lions ever seem to get a great coach? Other teams seem to be able to. Bill Belichick, Bill Parcells, Mike Shanahan, Bill Walsh, Joe Gibbs, Marv Levy, Mike Ditka, John Madden, Don Shula, Chuck Noll, Tom Landry, Bud Grant, and Vince Lombardi. All won Super Bowls or got their teams there more than once. What makes a coach great in the NFL? Hard to answer; you obviously need great players, but leadership and schemes are key.

NFL football is filled with injuries for all teams; thus, the reason it is necessary to have a 55-player roster. But it seems to us that the Lions have way more injuries than most teams. In 1982, to have 10 key players injured and then have Sims break his hand—what are the odds (see Appendix B)? These players were obviously injured in the preseason or in training camp. In 2003, the injury to Charles Rogers during practice hurt the team significantly (see Appendix F). His broken collar bone was re-injured in the first game this year and has cost him almost his entire first two seasons.

The Lions have lost games in the last minutes an incredible number of times. This is what tortures fans so much; they often seem so close to being good. Maybe the Vikings announcer was right on December 19th, 2004, when he said, "The Lions just don't think they can win."

I realize how often bad things happen around my birthday, which is October 26th. Chuck Hughes' death, Billy Sims' career cut short. Let's see what other memories the Lions have provided for my birthday week.

The Lions have always struggled with the red zone execution.

Inside your opponent's 20-yard line is where the game is won or lost offensively. The great teams score a lot of touchdowns from this position. The bad teams always seem to come close, but often have to settle for field goals. The NFL is a League that requires touchdowns to win. I would love to see the statistics on team field goals over the past 30 years. I am guessing the Lions have more than most teams. That is why we have had such successful kickers over the years: Errol Mann, Eddie Murray, and Jason Hanson. They had a lot of opportunities to kick field goals after drives stalled.

Let's look at the quarterbacks since 1965. Greg Landry was one of our best. I remember Bill Munson, Karl Sweetan, Milt Plum, Eric Hipple, Gary Danielson (one of our best), Chuck Long, Rodney Peete, Andre Ware, Erik Kramer (he won a playoff game—this makes him special), Scott Mitchell, Charlie Batch, Joey Harrington, and now Matt Stafford. I hope I'm not forgetting anyone. What happened to the days of Bobby Layne? I was in diapers when he was winning championships for Detroit. The only great Lions quarterback, and I missed it!

Why have the Lions struggled to get a great quarterback? Or, were these quarterbacks good, but were in a bad system, with bad coaching? None of them went on to greatness with other teams. Most of them never got a starting position again. Some never played in the NFL again. I guess our college scouting staff has never been very good. One could wonder what a great quarterback would do as a Lion? Let's dream for a moment and say the Lions had Peyton Manning as their QB next year. How about Tom Brady, Donovan McNabb, or Michael Vick? Is it the coach that makes the quarterback, or the quarterback that makes the coach? Or is it the offensive scheme, personnel, and leadership that are the keys? If we had one of these top QBs, would it be possible that the Lions would win 10 games next year? Why can't we seem to draft the right quarterbacks?

I often wonder about players' careers being determined in part by which team drafts them. What if Barry Sanders was drafted second that year by the Packers, instead of third by the Lions? Barry would have had several Super Bowl rings playing with Brett Favre. Could you imagine those two together? What if the Lions took Randy Moss instead of Terry Fair? What if they would have understood the potential of a young man playing football 30 miles from Detroit at the University of Michigan a few years ago? Why did New England take Tom Brady in the sixth round? They must have seen something in him. It's probably good for Brady that Detroit did not take him; who knows where his career would be today. I met Tom Brady when he was a 19-year-old at University of Michigan. He was working behind the counter at the U of M golf course and I recognized his name tag as the back-up QB at Michigan. I remember how young he looked. A very nice young man, I shook his hand and wished him luck in football—I think he did pretty well, what do you think?

The Lions just never seem to win close games. Their effort has always been solid, but there is no replacement for play makers and great coaching. We have had very few game-breaking types of players since 1957. The main ones have been Barry Sanders, Herman Moore, Charlie Sanders, Lem Barney, Mel Gray, Eddie Drummond, Al Baker, and Billy Sims. We have never had a quarterback that just willed us to victory. We have never had a coach that outsmarted the other coach. I would argue that the Lions have had some very good talent over these years but have had terrible head coaching. This is the reason they have lost so many games after leading at halftime. This is why they never seem to win the game in the fourth quarter of a close one. It seems it is a combination of poor strategy and a lack of leadership—neglecting to instill confidence and calm in the players at the most crucial times—that has led to failure.

Lions fans get so frustrated over games like the one against the Packers on October 25th, 1987 (see Appendix C). Green Bay jumps to a 24-0 lead, but the Lions fight back to take the lead 33-31 late in the game. The Packers kick a 45-yard field goal to go up 34-33, but the Lions keep fighting and drive the ball down in field goal position with a shot at winning the game. A 45-yard field goal attempt misses as time runs out. I'm guessing it was missed by Eddie Murray. Although we have had solid kickers over these torturous years, we have missed most big field goals to win games. Detroit has not been able to perform when it counts the most! Can you imagine how frustrating this game was for the players that killed themselves to come back, and never gave up, losing the game that way? Same story over 49 years; the offense takes the lead, the defense can't hold, and a missed field goal to lose. It has happened many, many times.

As I reviewed these games, the one that really stood out for me was the September 6th, 1992 loss to the Bears 27-24 on opening day. The day before, I broke my kneecap falling down a hill on a golf course (very athletic, I know). My orthopedic surgeon operated on me Sunday morning to put the bone back together with wire and two pins. It was very nice of Dr. Zeminik to come to work on a Sunday. I told him and the anesthesiologist that it was opening day for the Lions, and when given the choice of general anesthesia or a spinal for the operation, I chose the spinal. It was opening day for the Lions—a new season, a new hope. I didn't want to be sleeping after the surgery and miss the game. I also asked them if they could finish and get me back to the room by kickoff. I have always been a passionate Lions fan; does this prove it? I remember the Lions losing the game on the last play with one second to go. I was having such a great day!

Why are football fans so passionate? Why do Lions fans never give up the dream? Sport is one of the mainstays of "male bonding" in America. We go to the games with buddies, watch them together, and talk about them on the phone when life is too hectic to get together. Men don't talk about emotions, family, job satisfaction, or most other life matters. But when a team wins a professional or college championship, why do fans feel so much a part of it? It is the players who have killed themselves, preparing for years to experience that moment. It is their team, not ours. We must feel that they represent us, our city, or our universities. It speaks to the pride people have in the area they live in. For some people, it makes them feel special. They feel that they are part of something really big, and in their own small way they feel they were part of the championship, because they screamed and rooted their team on to victory. Some people have very low self-esteem and are not happy in their lives. For those few days or weeks, they are lifted to a different level and enjoy the adrenaline rush that can accompany a sports title. When the rush is over though, it's back to dealing with their lives and reality.

One of the major reasons football is the most popular sport in the United States is that only one game is played each week. Each game holds far greater importance than those in the other major sports. It is the ultimate team game—breakdowns in any area can prevent winning. What gives a team the ability to win the big one? To win a game that clinches a playoff spot, or one that sends you to the Super Bowl? I believe it is the head coach. They form the strategy for the game, call the plays, motivate the team, and make adjustments at halftime. Even Wayne Fontes, who took the Lions further than any other coach since 1957, had a terrible playoff record.

Sports as a hobby helped me through my teenage and young adult years more than anything, aside from my family. It provided a sense of passion in my life (while I was discovering women). It provided a healthy escape from stress. It teaches young people so many important values. It teaches you that life is competitive in the world of work and career. Sport teaches the importance of a team—the need to do your job with the greatest effort so others will also be successful. It teaches individual responsibility. It teaches kids to be good sports; not to rub it in when you win and how to accept losing without giving up on the next game. It teaches people to realize how far they can push themselves, accomplishing things they never thought they could. It gives you a sense of self-esteem and joy when you have had a great performance. Sports are an integral part of American culture.

It will be hard to forget the days after 9/11, when it was important to begin the healing process. President Bush walked on the field in Yankee Stadium to throw out the first pitch. He was wearing a bullet proof vest, and the Secret Service did not want him to be there. He showed courage and leadership that day. Sports brings people together to work for a common cause. We needed sports on that day. Few things can produce such passion and emotion.

Years ago, my buddy Woody heard a caller on a radio show. The caller was very depressed and told the host he was going to kill himself at 6:00 p.m. on Saturday. When the host asked why 6:00 p.m. Saturday, the guy said that he wanted to watch the Tigers game that afternoon. Sports do give people something to look forward to, even in the worst of circumstances.

The Tigers won two championships, in 1968 and 1984. The Red Wings won four from 1997 to 2008. The Pistons won three in 1988, 1989, and 2003. The University of Michigan won both basketball and football championships during that era, and Michigan State won two basketball championships. I was two years old when the Lions won their last championship in 1957. I don't remember it! Our Red Wings finally broke through winning the Stanley Cup in 1997 after 42 years without a championship. They had one of the best coaches in the history of sports in Scotty Bowman. The Lions have never had great coaches or quarterbacks, which are the two most important positions on an NFL team. I was too young to remember the one great quarterback we had, Bobby Layne. Buddy Parker was the coach from 1951 to 1956 and was part of our three championships. I would love to know why he resigned as coach on August 12th, 1957. He must have been considered our greatest coach. The game has clearly gotten more complicated since 1957. 1 think our best quarterbacks were Landry, Danielson, and Stafford. What would our team have been like if we ever had a Brett Favre, Peyton Manning, Dan Marino, or Joe Montana?

Am I being too hard on the Lions? They are not the only professional sports organization that has been bad for over 50 years. The Cubs in baseball, the L.A. Clippers and Cleveland Cavaliers in basketball, the Cardinals, Saints, and Browns in football have had similar histories. It's the nature of sports that some franchises never seem to be able to put a winning team together. The hope of improvement, the entertainment of the games, and the occasional great player who is worshipped, all serve the fans. And the dream that maybe one day we will play for a championship.

The term *fan* comes from the word *fanatic*. Clearly, too many people go overboard in their desire and emotional need for their team to win. You see it in fan behavior when too much drinking takes place, and when swearing and vulgarity are heard by kids. Why do so many people, particularly men, put so much into their teams? I believe it represents what is missing in a person's emotional life. People look for things in their lives to fill in missing holes. Troubled families, bad marriages, drinking or drug addictions, and disappointing careers all create a sense of emptiness. Others go about adult life with no passion. They are emotionally dead. Life has become too boring, too stressful, or both.

Other fans use sports as a healthy outlet and pause from adult routines. There is a magic about getting lost in a game. Time does not exist; problems are temporarily gone. The players and the teams are representing you and the city you live in. There is a deep sense of pride that people have in their teams.

How does a team like the Dallas Cowboys make it to eight Super Bowls? Dallas and Pittsburgh have the most appearances of any team. What is it about teams like San Francisco, Denver, Green Bay, Oakland, Miami, and New England that make them so successful? Do they know something the Lions don't? Are their owners wiser about football matters; have they hired better presidents or GMs? How do they recognize talent in coaches and players? I was recently reading a national football magazine with the cover story "The NFL's Greatest 100 Players." Were there any Lions? Nope. There was one honorable mention for

Shaun Rogers. Could that explain the terrible record of the past several years?

Being a Lions fan can be hazardous to your health. What happens to a fan when he has endured so much pain and suffering year after year? Depression sets in first. You find yourself a little down and discouraged most Sundays around 4:00 p.m. "I guess I'll get to those chores I've been putting off all weekend." As a kid, it meant ending the weekend on a downer—back to school tomorrow. As an adult, it's back to the work jungle on Monday morning. Listening to post-game shows and reading the sports section on Monday for the postmortem is a tradition. The radio announcer, Mark Champion, tries his best to be objective, but he has suffered as much as we have. You can tell that he is also a great fan of the Lions. The reflection in his voice after a particularly painful loss is obvious. There have been times I was worried that he might jump out of the booth! "Botched snap; game over."

After years of Sunday evening depression, a Lions fan may find himself not caring anymore, maybe not watching the whole game—just checking the score now and then. It is here that emotional distance and pulling away from the team takes place. "Who cares anyway, it's only a sport, I have more important things in my life to worry about. I'm not wasting my energy on them!" A fan with season tickets may begin thinking about not renewing them next year. You may start hoping that fans stay away in protest, so the team makes less money and begins to show the owners that we mean business. This is when the most toxic emotion begins to creep in—anger. Fans will take an incredible amount of poor performances and years of mediocrity. Why? Because of their intense need to escape the pressures of adult life. It's still one of the healthier ways to escape for a period of time.

As anger begins to set in sometime after year forty, the fan realizes that this is now serious. You begin ranting to your buddies about the Lions. "Can you believe how they lost Sunday?" You begin to say things like, "We could coach the team to 16 wins in four years." Wouldn't that be a great reality show? My buddy, who has been a successful high school football coach, and I take over the team for a year—we keep the offensive and defensive coordinators. How many games would the Lions win? Would we go 0-16? I have told friends that I thought we could win four to six games; am I nuts? I know people in Detroit would watch this reality show. George Plimpton would be proud!

Along with the anger and vowing to stop being a fan forever, delusions may begin to set in as the one described previously. "We could coach the team to four wins." I'm following through with my threat to not buy my season tickets next year. My friend's brother may want them—should I keep them in my name? What if they get good in the next few years? Am I being a disloyal fan? Maybe 50 years is too little time to give the team I love. I should be tougher and endure the pain until I'm 80 years old—only another 30 years!

Should the Lions begin putting the following warning on the back of their tickets? "Caution: Being a Lions fan for any prolonged period (20+ years) may lead to the following symptoms: depression, anger, rage, nausea, vomiting, delusions, and suicide. Check with your physician before committing to this team."

Can you imagine what it feels like to own a professional sports team? What it must feel like to be Mr. Ford or his son? How badly do they want to win a championship? What a great hobby to have, trying to put a football team together that becomes the best. I know it's a business, and the Lions have probably made a fair amount of money over the years. When a person runs the Ford Motor Company, he is probably doing pretty well financially. How much money does one man or family need? So, when I say it's an amazing hobby for the Fords, I think I'm right. The pride of winning a championship has got to mean more to the Fords than money. Does Mr. Ford feel like a failure? Certainly not in business, I'm sure. It has to get to him that he has tried everything he knows to give the city and the fans a winning team.

Our country is entertainment starved! We crave distractions from life constantly. I believe this is why people follow sports with such a passion. Too many people hate their work, are not happy in their relationships, and look for an escape from the stressful adult world in many ways. Some are healthier than others. When you watch your team on Sunday, you lose yourself completely. Your worries are gone, your problems can wait. Passion is the other key to following sports. People must have passion in their lives. Something that gets them exited, interested, motivated. Without passion, life can seem without meaning. People find their passions through careers, hobbies, relationships, family, money, sex, movies, theater, music, computers, and sports. Hollywood and sports represent huge entertainment, distraction, and money. Actors and athletes make unbelievable money: $20 million per movie; or $100 million per contract, like Michael Vick. NBA players can make $17 million a year, baseball players can get a 10-year, $250 million contract. Capitalism is a beautiful thing! I always wished I could get 50,000 people to pay $30 per ticket to watch me do a therapy session with a troubled client. Not exciting enough? I have several friends who are physicians and make a good living, but even this is not enough when they save a person's life! My old liberal beliefs are coming out, I apologize. Our priorities are a bit backwards in America, but it's the best system we've got.

I've been reading Charlie Sanders' new book, *Tales from the Detroit Lions*. When he played in 1962, he was making $16,000 a year. What has happened to the salaries, revenue, and business of sports is amazing. Do you think that athletes like Charlie Sanders resent the money these young men are making today? It seems that the multiyear contracts create some athletes who just coast. There is little incentive to get better. Although the level of talent is unbelievable today (training, weightlifting, nutrition, etc.), it seems we have a lot of "spoiled brats" who don't appreciate what they have. The distance and anger between fans and players that has occurred over the past 20 years is very predictable. When the average fan is making $40,000 a year at his or her job, and the average athlete is making $1 million or more per year, it has to affect how fans view athletes.

Terrell Owens was a perfect example of this. He was a spoiled brat who was always used to getting his way; throwing a tantrum because he felt he was underpaid by the Eagles. His contract was for $42 million over seven years! So, what does he do? He throws a fit and decides to be a bad boy, causing disruption of the team, causing chaos, and getting himself fired. The Eagles did the right thing.

We see some problems that have arisen from this insatiable need for stimulation and entertainment. There are so many choices today about how we spend our free time. The Internet, cable, video games, sports, movies, vacations, and hobbies are all available. We are on an adrenaline overload! You see it with young kids and teenagers. Most are able to be guided in the direction of maturity and responsibility in preparation for the adult world. Too many, however, get stuck in the entertainment, hedonistic world of play and avoidance of developmental growth. My son, when he was a teenager, was an example. His whole life was about entertainment. I was never a great disciplinarian, so some of the fault lies with his mother and me. But teens today have so much to choose from, it is amazing.

I believe that some of the passion has gone out of professional sports due to the amazing salaries. The average fan doesn't connect to the athlete or the team, because they just can't relate to their world. There is also a sense that athletes from earlier days were more loyal and dedicated to the cities and the sport than modern-day athletes. It seems that greed and money dominate. I believe some of this resentment towards professional athletes and entertainers was responsible for the NBA brawl in Detroit in November 2004, during a Pacers-Pistons game. For these reasons, many people are turning to high school and college sports to recapture the purity of the game. Young people playing for the thrill of competition and victory, representing their high school, college, or local team.

The NHL lockouts of 2004 and 2012 are other examples of problems in professional sports and how much of it has become strictly business. As a fan of hockey, I have been disgusted with the greed on both sides. Fighting about a salary cap; will it be $42 million or $49 million? My anger and that of many fans is that it comes down to an average NHL player saying, "I want my cap to allow me to make $1.4 million instead of $ 1 million." Owners have the risk of running a business, so I tend to support their side more for this reason. But in this case, I feel both sides are wrong. The owners can clearly hold out longer because they can sustain the losses more than the players. The players are starting to miss their paychecks. The average fan earns between $30,000 and $150,000 and has a hard time feeling bad for players fighting for an extra half-million dollars! We all have bosses or owners to deal with. I am a social worker in the public schools and make $84,000 per year with a Master's degree. Even though teachers get significant vacation time (so do pro athletes), their jobs are rather difficult. I believe that people resent the amount of money professional athletes make today, especially when you see some players with bad attitudes.

Let's look at two playoff games. The 1991 NFC championship game we lost to Washington and the 1993 playoff loss to the Packers. We had a great team in 1991; we were 12-4 and had just won our only playoff game since 1957. The reason to discuss this game has to do with the score at halftime. It was Washington 17-10. Thirty minutes of football left to get to the Super Bowl, and the Lions are down one touchdown. How does the team completely collapse and lose the second half, 24-0? It's coaching. Clearly, the Redskins were a great team, as they went on to win the Super Bowl, but they had a guy on the other sidelines named Joe Gibbs. We had Wayne Fontes.

My brother met Fontes at a bar one night near the Silverdome. He was very friendly and talked with my brother for over an hour about the Lions. Fontes told him that the problem with the team is that the offense scored too quickly. My brother thought that was a little strange. He was obviously talking about a ball control offense that eats up the clock and keeps guys like Brett Favre off the field. But, if you can score too quickly, you should be able to beat teams 49-21 every game. After Fontes left the bar, my brother talked to a personnel guy from the Lions, quite high up in the organization. He told my brother that they kept getting Fontes all these solid players, but that he was an "idiot" and didn't know how to use them. He did not care for Fontes, who of course we now know had the best results of any coach for the Lions since 1957. I wonder if it was because he was a such a good coach, or perhaps the results had more to do with a guy named Sanders!

The 1993 playoff loss to the Packers 28-24 on a last-minute 40-yard TD pass from Favre to Sterling Sharpe is another great example of complete and utter futility. We all remember Sharpe being wide open for the touchdown catch, not a Lions player within 20 yards of him. When it counts the most! What a great time for bad communication and a blown defensive coverage.

Reviewing these past seasons, I realize that passionate Lions fans have had only two exciting moments in the past 49 years. The first was the playoff win over Dallas in 1991. The second was watching Barry Sanders run throughout his career. This man was unbelievable, and I still feel bad for Barry that he was not drafted first by the Green Bay Packers the year he came out. He would have been wearing several Super Bowl rings to show the champion that he was!

Barry ran for two touchdowns on October 12th, 1997 against Tampa Bay of 80 yards plus; the only time this has ever been done in the NFL (see Appendix E). That year, he added another 80 plus yard touchdown run; three in one year—how amazing is that? In 1998, Barry ran for 150 yards plus in a game for the 25th time in his career, another all-time NFL record. He also had 15 runs of over 50 yards at that point in 1998; another all-time record. When Sanders retired, my heart went out of the Lions—I'm not sure I will ever get it back.

CHAPTER 9

The Year I Finally Snapped:
Was I Really Rooting Against the Lions?

IT'S DECEMBER OF 2004, AND THE SEASON JUST FINISHED a week ago, so the Lions' website doesn't have the game summaries yet. Let's see what sticks out from this season. We start strong, breaking the 24-game road losing streak in Chicago. Unfortunately, Charles Rogers' collar bone is also broken. There were two other great road wins at Atlanta and over the Giants. The 4-2 start got everyone excited. I was at the Washington game, which we lost to go to 4-4; a bad snap led to a blocked punt and TD, which was big. A crucial home game for Detroit, and the game, I believe, changed the season for Detroit. A win, and we would have been 5-3 the first half. It was also the most boring NFL game I have ever attended. A friend of mine from Pittsburgh agreed that it was the worst game he had ever seen. Other highlights include blowing leads at Minnesota of 19-7 and at Green Bay of 13-0. The missed extra point at home against the Vikings, which would have forced overtime, was classic. And then, to end the year right, the refs give the game to Detroit at home against the Bears on the worst call I have ever seen in the NFL. They can't even lose right! Now the Lions get the tenth pick in the draft instead of the fourth. We can't forget Jacksonville, when Eddie Drummond ran his second punt return back for a TD, forcing overtime and hardly anyone rushes Eddie to congratulate him—that's a good sign.

These past four years have been so painful for Lions fans, it is hard to describe. 16 wins in four years; what more can you say? The game of November 9th, 2003 was amazing. The Lions beat the Bears 12-10 while rushing for only 12 yards! Isn't that some kind of record? And to make it worse, the leading rusher was our receiver Reggie Swinton, who ran for nine yards on an end around. How can an NFL team run for 12 yards in a game? It's hard to believe they actually won this game.

Where do we go from here? I've decided to keep my two season tickets for one more year so I can have a chance at a ticket for Super Bowl XL. My mental illness must be creeping in; before, I said I was done with the team and canceling my season tickets. I have to find a good therapist; I happen to know several and will be glad to refer any distraught Lions fan who requires professional help. It is very understandable—a person actually has to be very strong to cope with the Lions since 1957.

Steve Mariucci said, "enough anguish," at his final press conference. I think he understands what this city has gone through with its football team over the years. Is he the guy to change things? Can he turn things around and get us to the Super Bowl? Although his coaching the first two years has been disappointing, he certainly comes across as a very bright, likable person. We are all pulling for you, Mooch!

It's January 8th, 2005—the NFL playoffs, how exciting! But where are the Lions? Oh, they didn't make the playoffs; there is always next year, right? I see ex-Lions players on other teams. Reuben Droughns from Denver, who rushed for over 1,200 yards this year; maybe the system helped him succeed. James Mungro of the Colts; he seems to be doing well—it might help to have your quarterback be Peyton Manning! Hey, there's Tom Moore, the offensive coordinator of the Colts, top offense in the League. Didn't he used to work for the Lions? There are many stories like this. The most amazing is when Don Shula was an assistant coach on the Lions. Didn't he end up having a good career?

The announcers are saying that it has been a long time since Denver has won a playoff game, all the way back to 1998 when they won their back-to-back Super Bowls. Don't we feel sorry for them?

It's the week of January 24th, 2005. It will be the Eagles and the Patriots in the 39th Super Bowl in Jacksonville. I don't see how the Eagles can win this game, but you never know. Tom Brady will attempt to run his record to 9-0 in the playoffs; absolutely incredible. Of course, the Lions talk continues. Should the Lions trade Williams or Rogers and a draft pick for Randy Moss? Detroit has hired its new offensive coordinator, a 64-year-old friend of Steve Mariucci from the 49'ers. The 49'ers had one of the worst offenses in the League the last few years, and last year was 2-14; the worst record in the NFL. It seems the League is a "good ol' boys' network." Marc Trestman was available and very well thought of, but he clearly wasn't smart enough for the Lions. It seems that Mariucci has brought in a coach that will be an aide to him—obviously Mariucci wants to call the offense himself. This coach will probably retire in a few years; why don't the Lions ever seem to hire the right people? If the next two seasons don't show significant improvement, Millen, Mariucci, and Harrington will probably all be gone.

I have settled down after the season ended three weeks ago in January 2005. I don't hate the Lions anymore. I do believe they have a legitimate chance of winning nine or 10 games next year. It's not my delusions talking, is it? Part of the illness has to do with going through a recovery period a month after the season is over, and then having the delusions return. I need to see my shrink soon. I am getting healthy—I am recognizing the symptoms of relapse. By July, all of the horrible memories of the last 48 years will have faded. Fans will be ready to predict a playoff season for our beloved Lions. The hope of a new season is always exciting; the problem has always been when they have to play the games. It's like a death and a re-birth. Fans never stop hoping, no matter how realistic it is or isn't.

Today's sports talk radio subject, in February 2005, from Tony Ortiz is about what will demand more attention on September 11th, 2005; the Tigers in a pennant race or the opening game of the NFL season for the Lions? As much as Detroit would love a successful baseball season, there is no question that Ortiz is correct when he says that the NFL rules in Detroit. This is a city that is obsessed with its football team, much like the Eagles fans who lost the Super Bowl two days ago. The ex-mayor of Philadelphia recently said that if the Eagles were to lose the NFL championship game two weeks ago for the fourth consecutive year, there would be no one going to work on Monday, because the streets would be filled with the dead bodies of Eagles fans who had jumped! Detroit has a similar passion. I can't imagine what this town would be like if we ever made it to the big game.

We talk about the Lions 365 days a year. NFL football is by far the dominant sport in this country. The Pistons might be the next most talked about because of their recent championship.

The Lions signed two players yesterday. It's official, we're going to the Super Bowl! These are the two players who will put us over the top; the players we have been waiting 47 years for since our last championship. Seriously, they were two solid signings that should improve the team. They signed a hard-hitting safety and a reliable tight end. This will allow the team more flexibility with their first-round pick at number 10 to take a player other than a safety. The sports talk shows are buzzing! The safety, Kennedy, was reportedly at the airport about to go interview with the Miami Dolphins when the Lions closed the deal; I hope he doesn't regret not getting on that plane; maybe not today, but . . . does he understand the history of our Lions?

Is it possible my Lions-induced delusions are coming back? I'm actually starting to feel some hope for next season. The players they signed this week in March of 2005, along with an expected signing of a solid back-up quarterback, has got me thinking 10 wins and a playoff appearance. We are also getting Charles Rogers back, hopefully Boss Bailey, and the 10th pick in the draft. The anger over last season is starting to go away. This is the life of a Detroit Lions fan; sometime within a month or two of the Super Bowl, we begin to have hope. This is because we are six months away from opening day and have no chance of losing yet.

I probably should make an appointment with a therapist, since these delusions of success with the Lions can return quickly. I must return to the reality of the past 48 years, shouldn't I? It is a lot of fun to fantasize and pretend that we will win, though. What's wrong with living in a fantasy world?

There is big news about Mark Champion losing his spot as the Lions' announcer. I have a lot of mixed feelings about this. He is a great announcer with a tremendous voice. You can tell that he loves the Lions as he was calling the games; when the Lions lost a heart breaker, as they often did, you could hear the pain in his voice. He reflected what tortured Lions fans were feeling. I have told friends that I was worried that Champion would jump out of the booth after some particularly hard losses. He became more critical of the team in recent years, with good reason. His honesty was warranted. He has been the voice of the Lions for 16 years, and Lions football won't be the same without him. If the Lions ever have any success, it won't feel right without Mark Champion. Talk about someone who has suffered through the tough times with this team. Maybe he will get the play by play of another NFL team and he will get to see what real football looks like! He is also the radio announcer for our world champion Detroit Pistons, so someone can still recognize his talents.

Mike McMahon signed a two-year deal with the Eagles. Good for him; I met him twice, a very nice guy. I was upset last year when Harrington was playing poorly, and they thought so little of McMahon that they did not play him. I felt there was no reason to sign a back-up who was only going to play if there is an injury. A third-string quarterback can do that. Now we wait to see if the Lions sign Brad Johnson or Jeff Garcia as the back-up who will compete for the starting job with Harrington. Both of these quarterbacks are at the end of their careers. If they were really still good, do you think their teams would have let them go? The 48-year problem of poor quarterbacking for the Lions continues, with no end in sight.

The Lions signed Jeff Garcia to a one-year contract to compete with Joey Harrington for the QB position. Garcia has had two poor years and is 35 years old; he was in the pro bowl three years while in San Francisco playing for Mariucci. His receivers those years were Jerry Rice and Terrell Owens—I think that might have something to do with his success. Anyway, it was considered a good signing. Someone should let Garcia know his career is over and he will be going out without a Super Bowl ring. Does he know anything about the last 48 years in Detroit? The next big date for Lions junkies is at the end of April when we take the 10th pick in the draft, and try to find that "Tom Brady" quarterback late in the rounds who we can develop when it's obvious that Joey is a bust.

Dre' Bly was quoted in the paper on March 22nd, 2005, as saying that it is time for the players to step up and win this year. No more blaming the organization or the coaches. He said he came to Detroit because he believed in Steve Mariucci, and this is the year to win, especially with the Super Bowl in Detroit. Does that mean he thinks the Lions should make it to the Super Bowl this year? Very inspiring, don't you agree?

The sports talk show discussed a report that the Lions will be meeting with the quarterback out of Utah this week because there is a chance he may be available at the 10th pick in the draft. Most likely, he will be taken before, but just in case. The discussion centered around the question of why the Lions would consider drafting a quarterback; especially with the first pick. There was a sense that if they took this guy, they might decide to cut Joey Harrington because they want to avoid a large bonus that is due to him by June. Garcia would then be the starter while they develop the college kid. It's April and we are talking football! As the host of the show said, "Anytime there is news about the Lions, it becomes the first thing you need to talk about."

It turns out that the Lions' management basically lied to the media about the Utah quarterback. They said that a tight end out of Stanford with the same first and last name (Alex Smith) was in for an evaluation. After a week or so, the media found out that both players were in for an interview; the tight end and the quarterback. Why would the Lions lie to the media? People believe the Lions were trying to protect Harrington's "fragile ego." I don't understand how this organization does business.

It is nine days before the 2005 NFL draft on April 14th, 2005. The sport radio shows are talking Lions today since their schedule was released for this year. The disturbed, delusional fans were calling in with predictions of 10, 11, and even a 12-win season. This disease can creep up on a person very quickly, without warning. It is sad that so many fine Detroit people suffer from this incurable illness. I must discover a cure for this problem.

Draft day is two days away. The Lions may take a very fast, physical linebacker out of Texas. There has been a lot of talk about taking a quarterback from Florida State, McPherson, in the third round. He had some problems that involved jail time, but as long as he can throw a ball and win games.... This is a very exciting time for Lions fans; a time when hope is at its highest. I have to admit that even I believe this should be a good year for the Lions. Will this change when they actually have to play the games in September?

The draft was Saturday. It was our Super Bowl. If you heard the callers on the sports radio shows, you heard the excitement only a draft day can bring a Lions fan. This is as good as it gets.

We pick Mike Williams out of USC—a huge, fast wide receiver. I have to admit that I was also excited and surprised that he dropped to the 10th pick. The three receivers the Lions have are outstanding and should score a lot of points if Charles Rogers stays healthy and our QB can get them the ball. As much as I have given up on this team, I have to say that they should win nine or 10 games and get to the playoffs this year. It is a realistic goal. The pressure is on Harrington and Mariucci at this point. Most of the pressure is on Mariucci, since Garcia will be the QB if Joey can't get it done. If only we didn't have to play the games—we always look better on paper!

The yearly cycle of a Lions fan is like the mourning process itself. The hope is there from draft day in April through the first game in September. As the games are played and the reality of the Lions' history repeats itself, depression sets in. After the initial depression, the anger comes out at mid-season when it becomes obvious that we will have the same results as always. After the season, the anger holds on from December through March—it goes along with the dreariness of our cold, bleak winters in Detroit. When April arrives, the hope of spring, better weather, and draft day erases the pain we have struggled with since September. The cycle repeats itself each year.

The talk about the Lions has been non-stop for the past four days since the draft. Some people say that we are crazy for the Lions. I'm not so sure about that. If anything, we are crazy because of the Lions! The Pistons are in the playoffs with an excellent chance at repeating as NBA champions, and 90 percent of the talk is about the Lions.

I have again become one of the fans who is really looking forward to September. I may never give up on this team; I think it's because we know what it might feel like should we ever win the championship. Without question, it would be the biggest sports thrill of my life, and that of millions of Lions fans throughout the country.

Almost a week after the draft, the Lions talk continues on the sports shows. The question today was, should Matt Millen be given a new contract after his expires this year? Most people said yes, because there is a feeling that he has done a great job the past few years in the draft. The one that might cost him his job was the Harrington draft four years ago. After this week, I'm sure things will die down until training camp in July. We open at home against the Packers, play the Bears on the road, and then have a bye in week three. We should know by then if Harrington will be the guy during week four, or if Garcia will be put in to take over. The Lions are one of the great things about fall in Michigan.

Spindler says the only acceptable outcome this season is the team making the playoffs and winning a playoff game. I agree. Making the playoffs is simply not good enough. What might be equally important to fans is starting to play exciting football again. Aside from all the losing, the games have been almost unwatchable. When Barry Sanders played, games were exciting whether we won or lost. The Lions talk might die down as the draft is one week removed, and the Pistons get further into their championship run.

The Lions had their mini-camp this past weekend, with all the draft choices in. This is like Super Bowl week in Detroit. All you see and hear about on sports shows is the improved team the Lions have this year. Roy Williams made a spectacular catch with one hand; the ball was underthrown and he caught it with his one hand and trapped it on his back. It was an amazing catch. Shut it down for the season, this is as good as it might get. No one of course mentioned that Joey completely underthrew the ball and it was a terrible pass! We will see what kind of coach Steve Mariucci is.

They are still talking Lions on the sports radio stations around Detroit, two weeks after the NFL draft. The question to the fans was which of the three young receivers will have the best year: Charles Rogers, Roy Williams, or Mike Williams. Most people think it will be Roy Williams. I believe that football has become the national pastime, overtaking baseball.

It is May 12th, 2005, and Matt Millen is considering making an offer to Ty Law, the ex-U of M all-pro cornerback, who has championship rings with the Patriots. He is recovering from foot surgery, but Millen feels you can't have too many cornerbacks. We will see if we can land him; I'm thinking the Patriots let him go for reasons beyond the salary cap. I can't wait until August when the preseason games begin. There will be a great deal to write about this season; I think the boys will give me enough material to finish this book. If the season goes poorly, as most of the last 48 have, then there will be many more "I don't believe it" moments to write about. I hope the luck and history of this franchise turns around so I can write about the miracles of the 2005-2006 season.

There was a leak on the sports radio show about a contest that was completed this past week by EA Sports for a skills competition to be aired on July 16th, 2005. Joey Harrington was one of seven quarterbacks in the competition; guess which place he came in? Last place. And the quarterbacks were not the top quarterbacks in the NFL. No Culpepper, Favre, Brady, Vic, or

Manning. Joey comes in last! Could that be connected to the Lions' 16-48 record for the last four years? A funny piece on Harrington recently suggested that he change his name from Joey to Joe. This might inspire an image of greater leadership. We don't remember "Joey" Namath, "Joey" Montana, or "Joey" Schmidt.

The odds are out for the 2006 Super Bowl; the Lions are 42:1 odds to win. The sports radio show pointed out that every one of the NFL teams are considered a better chance to win it, including the top seven college teams! Of course, the Lions probably don't have the worst odds; some team is probably 100:1. We never get any respect around the country.

Big news! Charles Rogers was allowed to take off his red shirt and put on a blue shirt. This means he can take contact during the mini camps. The red shirt indicated that he was not to be hit due to the concern of his two broken collar bones the last two seasons. This was discussed on sport radio off and on throughout the day.

CHAPTER 10

The Top 20 "I Don't Believe It" Moments from 1970-2021

THERE ARE SO MANY "I DON'T BELIEVE IT" MOMENTS, IT WAS hard to narrow it down to the Top 20. Some of these are not really moments but amazing records or streaks. Anyway, here is my top 20 since 1970:

20. Botched snap, missed extra point against the Vikings, 2004. I will never forget this one! After it happened, I went to my computer and began writing this book.

19. The 16-game losing streak to the Redskins in the 1980s and 1990s. It is hard to believe you can lose that many in a row to one team, but the Redskins were great in those days.

18. The 13-game losing streak to the Vikings in the 1970s. Here is another team that found every possible way to beat the Lions. You could have 20 "I Don't Believe It" moments just with the Vikings.

17. Sterling Sharpe's TD catch uncovered losing a playoff game to the Packers in 1993. We had just beaten the Packers the week before at home to end the season. Not a good time for

a blown coverage; Sharpe didn't have a Lion defender within 20 yards of him.

16. The 24-road-game losing streak from 2000-2003. Absolutely amazing! It was hard to believe that the Lions could lose every road game played for three years straight. I think this record may stand forever.

15. Two-point attempts in Arizona by Bobby Ross, down 23-19, in 1999. He tried for two two-point conversions, saying he didn't want to play for overtime because of the Arizona heat.

14. December 21st, 1997: Reggie Brown almost dies on the field against the Jets, the same day Barry Sanders rushes for over 2,000 yards. Was I really watching a second Lion die on the field? A strange game of highs and lows: Sanders over 2,000 yards, Brown's medical crisis, and the Lions clinching the playoff spot.

13. The Lions win the overtime coin toss with Chicago in a 2002 game, but Marty Mornhinweg decides to kick, giving Chicago the ball, because he believed having the wind in their favor was more important than having the ball. He was wrong. The Bears scored a field goal without the Lions ever having the ball. I was stunned to see him give the Bears the ball, even with a huge wind. I had never seen that in an NFL game. Has it happened before or since?

12. The 23-20 loss to Chicago, preventing playoffs, Edinger field goal, and start of Millen era in 2000. Charlie Batch re-injured his ribs at the end of the game. The Bears took great satisfaction keeping us out of the playoffs. Edinger was the kicker from Michigan State—how ironic. Batch said that if he hadn't gotten hurt that game, Millen may have never come in, and he may not have signed with the Steelers and walked away with a ring for Super Bowl XL in Detroit.

11. The 23-20 loss to Tampa Bay in 1988. "What does a coach have to do around here to get fired?" Darryl Rogers asks, one of the boldest things I have ever heard in sports. Again, this loss kept us out of the playoffs.

10. Eddie Murray misses a field goal against the 49'ers, preventing the NFC championship in 1983. We all remember Monte Clark praying to the heavens. When Murray missed wide right, it was a sick feeling. We had a golden opportunity to play in the NFC championship game.

9. The 5-0 playoff loss at Dallas in 1970. I loved Greg Landry and Lem Barney. This was one of the best teams we have had in the past 50 years. We remember the safety—we should have won that game.

8. A fan is roughed up at Ford Field for holding a "Fire Millen" sign in 2005. I was at this one, but left before all the commotion and saw it on the news later. This day will be remembered as one of the most embarrassing and worst in Lions history.

7. "Miracle in Motown" on December 3, 2015, when Aaron Rogers wins the game with no time left on the clock, throwing a Hail Mary 61-yard pass to Richard Rogers. It was voted the NFL Play of the Year by The ESPY Awards.

6. Justin Tucker of the Baltimore Ravens kicks an NFL record 66-yard field goal to beat the Lions 19-17 on September 26, 2021.

5. November 17th, 1991: Mike Utley is paralyzed at the Silverdome. What a sad day in Lions history. It shows how dangerous this NFL game is. I am surprised more players don't get paralyzed with the speed of the game and the number of violent collisions. Utley has been a very courageous man, making progress with his mobility and raising money and awareness for patients with spinal cord injuries. We will

never forget his "thumbs up" as he was carried off the field that day.

4. Barry Sanders retires, 1999. My disappointment and disbelief over this were intense. It was not only the end of an era we may never see again, but I so wanted to see Barry break the all-time rushing record. He had so much respect for Walter Payton that he did not want to displace him. Playing for the Lions has also taken its toll on him. That is understandable. It can destroy an athlete's energy.

3. Three calls/no calls by refs that cost the Lions a win:

A. Calvin Johnson's last-minute touchdown catch to win the game is overturned by officials in Chicago during the opening game in 2010. The referee explained that Johnson did not "complete the process of the catch." Lions fans were shocked and sickened by the worst call I have ever seen in the NFL. The League looked foolish that day.

B. January 5, 2015, at Dallas for the playoffs... a flag was thrown for pass interference on a 3rd down and 1 for the Lions, and then "without explanation," the flag was picked up. It likely cost the Lions their first playoff win since 1991. To make things worse, Dean Glandena, the VP of officiating for the NFL, was seen on the Dallas party bus in August of the previous year, with the son of the owner, Jerry Jones. This is strictly prohibited as a conflict of interest. Glandena received no discipline from the League. For too many years, our Lions received no respect and were screwed by the refs regularly.

C. October 5, 2015 . . . Seattle 13-10 win over Detroit. A no call after Seattle bats the ball out of the end zone. It should have been Lions ball, first down on the 1-yard line.

2. October 24th, 1971: Chuck Hughes' death on the field at Tiger Stadium. This was the saddest day in the history of Lions football, the only time a player has died on the field during an NFL game. I was at the game and heard about his death when I got home.

1. The 63-yard field goal by Tom Dempsey in 1970. This book starts out with my memory of watching this game at my buddy Woody's house in Detroit. When we saw the ball go through to win the game for New Orleans, the title of my book was born: "I Don't Believe It."

CHAPTER 11

The 2005 Season Diary: "Can You Believe It?"

SHOULD IT BE JOEY OR JEFF? AFTER TWO EXHIBITION GAMES of the 2005 preseason, most are saying Joey, because he is 15 of 16 with a quarterback rating of 107. I say Jeff, because he has led the team on its only touchdown, and he has a great ability to escape a rush and can run. We will see by game four of the regular season. The young receivers look great; Rogers is healthy. The defense looks bad; the team looks like the same old Lions, but it's hard to say during the preseason.

It's *Monday Night Football* against the Rams in the preseason. Al Michaels, John Madden, and our new black jerseys. Big time in the Motor City: our Lions get to showcase their new team and the stadium that will host Super Bowl XL. The starters should play two or three quarters. Next February, will we be able to say, "I don't believe it, the Lions are in the Super Bowl"? I don't think so, but it would be the ideal ending for this book.

37-13 Rams on Monday night preseason, and it was "worse than that" as the morning sports talk shows described the game. I guess the Lions weren't "ready for some football." I was at this masterpiece, and when I saw the Lions coming on to the field through a cloud of smoke in their new black uniforms, I said I hoped that wasn't the highlight of the night. It was. The new uniforms were great—I like the look. The play on their field looked very familiar, however. The third exhibition game is supposed to be the dress rehearsal for the start of the season in two weeks; let's hope it doesn't reflect the ability of this team. John Madden would say that the Rams looked like they were playing against a Pop Warner team in this one.

The offense and defense were both horrible. Special teams played well. Let's review some of the highlights. The opening drive was a three and out. There were two incomplete passes by Harrington and a three-yard run. The first play for the Rams was a 64-yard run. The Rams did whatever they wanted all night; receivers wide open—they ran at will. There were a lot of excuses after the game for Joey Harrington because the offensive line played so poorly, resulting in at least four sacks at key times. I don't want to hear the excuses; I do not believe Harrington has what it takes to lead this team and be successful. He is similar to Darko Milicic of the Pistons—a very high draft choice who is probably going to be a bust. His three and out got the team off to a very bad start. Later, in the red zone, the Lions run the ball in for a TD but are flagged for not one but two holding penalties. Back to the 25-yard line; Harrington makes two throws on second and third down. The first was three yards and incomplete and the second was seven yards and dropped by Pollard. They did not even attempt to throw the ball into the end zone. Is that Harrington or Mariucci? At a key point in the game, we go for it on fourth down and half a yard when the score was 21-6. A touchdown puts us right back in the game. They run right up the middle, fooling no one, and we lose a yard and turn the ball over on downs. Was that Mariucci or Harrington? Was it Ted Tollner or Harrington?

In the third quarter, Garcia takes over as QB; I am looking forward to him proving me right with my buddy, after I tell him that Garcia is the better of the two quarterbacks. His first play results in two Lions penalties—illegal receiver down field and intentional grounding! I don't believe it!

We shouldn't overreact to this loss. I liked how the players handled it after the game, and I also thought Mariucci handled it well when he said that he was "alarmed" by the performance. He should be alarmed. I do not have much confidence in our head coach. He is clearly a very well-spoken, likable guy, but he has not been effective in his first two years here. I still believe that Garcia will end up as the starter, because he sees the field better and runs well at key times. Harrington has no touchdowns in three games; not a good sign. Our backup QBs have both thrown TD passes with the second and third units in.

My friend and I even commented on all the other things that went wrong on this night; a serious neck injury to a Rams player delayed the game for 20 minutes; the overhanging camera coming down on the field had to be corrected; and the offensive statistics were added wrong for both teams at halftime. When dealing with the Lions, you never know what to expect. Well, you know not to expect championship football since 1957.

I think everyone is overestimating the talent that Matt Millen has brought to the team. The coaching and quarterbacking are so poor that they destroy any talent that we may be able to show. They are an interesting team; you can't be surprised if they win nine or 10 games; and you can't be surprised if they win five or six. We will start the story on September 11th against the Packers. A Packers fan held a sign at last night's game saying, "You're going down Lions on Sept. 11th—The Messenger." We will soon find out.

The last exhibition game in Buffalo—a disaster. Jeff Garcia breaks his leg! They are in trouble now. Some of my friends with season tickets are not optimistic. One guy says, "I'm giving up my season tickets after this year if they don't make the playoffs." The Lions actually won the game and looked good. The third string (now second string) quarterback, Dan Orlovsky, played quite well for a rookie. He looks like he has good potential. It comes down to two key people to determine the success of the year: Joey Harrington and Steve Mariucci. If things don't go well, it could get ugly at Ford Field. I will be there Sunday when they open the season against the Packers. God help us.

On the Internet I noticed an article on the most valuable teams in the NFL; the Lions were listed at 18 out of 32 teams. A 44th percentile ranking compared to the value of all the other teams—that's just about the same as their winning percentage the past 49 years. I was surprised the value wasn't higher. The Washington Redskins were number one and the Minnesota Vikings were last at 32. I have to do something with my time while I wait for the big season opener!

Three days until the opener. I will be there with my buddies. I'm not as excited as I used to be, probably because I don't expect much out of the Lions this year. I am predicting an 8-8 season this year. The older I get (I am turning 50 this year), the less into sports I am. As a young man I had a sense of ease about life; a sense that life was simple. As I experienced some of the more difficult things about adult life, my perspective on the importance of sports changed. Becoming a father, going through two divorces, and managing a career over 25 years has changed me. I understand what is really important in life. Sports are not one of those things. That doesn't mean that I don't take pleasure in losing myself in sports; I still do. It's just on a different level. I am a huge pro basketball fan and very passionate about our Pistons. It's because they recently won a championship. I'm sure if the Lions ever got that good, I would be a crazy fan again. I think part of it is that I really believe I am facing reality with the Lions and accept the strong possibility that they will never be good until ownership changes.

The Lions earn a 17-3 victory over the Packers on September 11th, 2005. You must give the Lions, Harrington, and the defense credit for this win. Harrington was steady with two TD passes, no interceptions, and a rating in the 90s. The defense was the best I have seen it in years. Kennedy's interception tip to Holt was fantastic. The pass coverage was excellent. The Lions got a huge break that changed the game when a completion on a bomb down to the Lions' three-yard line was called back for offensive pass interference. On that play, the Packers top receiver went down for the year with an ACL injury. If they score that touchdown to tie the game, there was a very real risk of losing.

The headlines in the paper said "Undefeated"; "Super Bowl or Bust!" Aren't we overreacting just a little bit? There is one little problem with this optimism—there are 15 games left to be played. Last year's 4-2 start ended ugly, losing eight of the last 10 games. Why don't we wait until they play half of their games before we get too excited? This team has ripped my heart out many times; I have learned to be cautious. On the other hand, the optimism is warranted. The Lions looked better than they have in a long time. Their division is weak, so there is a legitimate chance of winning the North. Are my delusions coming back again?

Back to reality in game two, when *Detroit Free Press* headlines said: "Can't Bear to Watch! Lions Clawed 38-6" and "Lions Mauled by Bears 38-6." On the sports radio show they are having callers spin "the Lions wheel of mediocrity." It was another horrible performance that looked a lot like the preseason loss to the Rams a few weeks ago on *Monday Night Football*. The trouble began when our substitute kicker, Remy Hamilton from U of M, missed an extra point after a nice TD pass from Harrington to Roy Williams, which appeared to tie the game at seven. His one moment in the NFL at age 31, and he can't convert an extra point. I guess his NFL career will be considered a disappointment.

Everything caved in from there. A 73-yard punt return for a touchdown; an interception return for a touchdown; five Harrington interceptions; 28 yards rushing by the Lions compared to 186 by the Bears. Once again, the Lions make Kyle Orton look like a seasoned pro in his second NFL game. The two other moments that stand out were when Roy Williams turned the wrong way on a pattern in the end zone, resulting in an easy interception for Chicago. When he got to the bench, he got into a shouting match with Kevin Jones. The final symbolic straw was when the Lions go for it on the fourth and one in the second half, and Harrington and Jones collide on the hand off, losing three yards. One of the sports shows said it best: "You look for consistency and improvement and we see neither in this team."

Now, I said I won't judge Harrington and the Lions until they have played eight games this year, and I am sticking to that promise. The Bears looked very good, and they may be the best team in the North this year. I must say at this point, though, that our offensive line is terrible. They don't open holes in the run game, and they give Joey only two seconds to throw the ball. I challenge anyone to find a worse line in the NFL. This division may be won this year with seven or eight wins, which means you are always in it in the North. The problem is, even if the Lions win the division with seven to nine wins and go to the playoffs, they will get killed in the first round. I still cannot believe that Mr. Ford gave Millen a five-year extension to be the Lions president, after having the worst record in the NFL his first four years. I do believe at this point he will have no choice but to fire Mariucci if the team does not win at least seven games. Peter King of the national media noted that "Joey looked like a piranha on the sidelines," with no one going near him. He interpreted this to represent a lack of respect by teammates.

As an example of how crazy Detroit is about the NFL and the Lions, look no further than the sports talk shows the next day. "I can't take them anymore; they are terrible...." This after my alma mater Michigan State had a huge win at Notre Dame on Saturday, 44-41 in overtime, resulting in their national ranking of number 17 this week in college football. They eventually got to that game after an hour of doom and gloom discussion about the "kittens."

On the cover of the NFL preview magazine, the headline read, "How the Lions Won the Super Bowl"—in the "pigs fly" edition. The fan predictions for this year included the following: (1) 7-9, there should still be a good receiver left when their drafting number 12 next year; (2) 9-7, the Lions will sneak into the playoffs, where they will be annihilated 45-0. However, this will be seen as progress, and the M&M boys will be rewarded with contract extensions; (3) 9-7, the Lions will make the play offs and lose. Any better than that and I'll eat my shorts; (4) 13-3, the season will culminate with a Super Bowl victory. Note: this prediction was made after taking a prescribed medication that has euphoria as a side effect. (4) 8-8, based on some lucky breaks. Super Bowl? They have about as much chance to play in it as I do.

The Lions have a bye in week three and will not play for two weeks until they travel to Tampa Bay on October 2nd. Tampa is 2-0. Every day on the sports talk shows, you hear hours of Lions analysis. The offensive line, Harrington, the defense, the coaches, the draft picks... it never stops. People are obsessed with the NFL, and Detroit is obsessed with the Lions. I am sure they will be discussed daily until they play their third game. These two weeks will seem to take forever. I am looking forward to the next chapter with the Lions. Will they continue their horrible play, or reverse things? History would suggest the former, but you never know!

Our Lions are all alone in first place at 1-1, how about that! Chicago had to play a real NFL team this week, the Bengals, and were beaten 24-7. The Vikings finally won, beating the Saints 33-16, and the Packers go to 0-3 by losing to the Bucs 17-16. The other three North teams are 0-3, 1-2, and 1-2. The record for the North is 3-8. There is no question in my mind that nine wins will take the division, most likely eight wins, with an outside shot at seven. Could six wins take this division? It seems impossible, but you never know. These are four bad football teams. The Lions are already a six-point underdog at Tampa this Sunday.

There are three days before Sunday and the third game of the season. Not as much talk on the radio this week about the Lions because of the Michigan-Michigan State game on Saturday. After this weekend, the sports radio shows will once again be filled with Lions talk. Jeff Garcia will probably be able to play by the sixth game of the season. If Harrington has played poorly, I'm sure he will be the starter. It is difficult to know if Garcia has what it takes to win. The Lions have so many weaknesses; quarterback is just one of them. The biggest problem for this team is the offensive line and the coaching. I'm going to see the game on my girlfriend's dad's new 62" high-definition TV. I wonder if they will look better on a high-def screen.

They still look bad, even on a great TV. Actually, the Lions gave a very solid effort—the defense was great except for two big TD passes. The offense was horrible until the last four minutes of the game, when Harrington led the team down the field and threw an apparent game-winning touchdown. Was Pollard in bounds? "I don't believe it!" The play is reversed by the re-play official, and the Lions lose. I thought he was out of bounds on the re-play they showed—later that night, in slow motion, it was clearly a touchdown. The Lions got screwed! They should be 2-1 instead of 1-2. The other horrible play was a defensive holding by Goodman that reversed an interception by Detroit. Two bad calls by the officials that both went against the Lions. Tampa wins 17-13 over Detroit. Tampa had four turnovers and we still couldn't beat them. The Lions had 145 yards of offense and only six first downs going into the last drive in the fourth quarter with just over five minutes left in the game.

On the NFL show, they had a comedy skit about the NFC North division. They said the NFL rules would be changed for them and would let them end a play by two hand touch on defense. They said that if you could spell Mariucci's name correctly, you could be the Lions' quarterback. The last dig said that Detroit gets to bring real Lions on the field with them for games. Our division is bad; 3-10 as of today. And two of the wins were against each other!

I am actually starting to feel bad for Harrington. The kid looked so depressed after this game. Even when he does something right, it doesn't go his way. It is clear that Garcia will be the QB in three weeks when he gets healthy, although that will not guarantee success either. The good news is that the Lions are tied for first with Chicago at 1-2. I really believe that the winner of the North will have six to eight wins. I will be surprised if any team has nine or more.

Green Bay goes to 0-4, and the North is now 3-11 this year. More good news for the Lions; Charles Rogers, the second pick in the draft three years ago, has been suspended for four games due to drug use. It was the third test he has failed. What else can go wrong for the Lions? You know there will be more.

The Lions beat Baltimore 35-17 on October 9th, 2005, to go to 2-2 for the year. I was out of town on a golf trip (where I got my first hole in one), so I didn't see the game. Baltimore had 21 penalties, which was the second highest total in NFL history. Our defense played very well. Harrington was 10-23 for 97 yards with one TD and two interceptions. It was another poor performance by Joey. I am sure that as soon as Garcia recovers from his leg injury, he will be the starter for the Lions. That should be three games from now in Cleveland.

On talk radio this week, one of the topics was if Mariucci should be fired. I find this strange the week after they won a game. The truth is the Lions would be 3-1 if they were not robbed by an official's call in Tampa Bay. They are in first place in their division; Chicago is 1-3, Minnesota is 1-3, and Green Bay is 1-4. Our division is 5-12 overall. The other big story is our receiver Roy Williams making negative comments obviously directed at Harrington. The shows are making fun of the Lions by playing music from *Days of Our Lives*. I am surprised there is so much controversy the week after a win. It must be that a lot of people, including the players, are not fooled by their first-place position. Everyone seems to be waiting for a typical Lions collapse. Will it come, or maybe the question is, when will it begin?

"Oh, my," as Mark Champion used to say; Carolina 21-20 over the Lions with a TD pass with 32 seconds left. The kick is returned by McQuarters to the 50-yard line, but Joey goes 0-4 passing and cannot get the team to the 35-yard line for a chance to win. It was pathetic. On a day when the defense hit harder than I have seen a Lions team hit in 20 years, get four turnovers, including two TD returns off of interceptions, they still lose. It was as though we had no offense on the field. The defense outscores the offense 14-6. I thought the best idea was to refuse the ball and force Carolina to play offense the whole game. Even though Harrington threw for over 200 yards, which is a big day for him, I believe his career is over as a Lion. As soon as Garcia is ready, which should be two weeks, the change will be made.

The talk shows continue to play the theme song from *Days of Our Lives*, calling it "Days of the Lions." Joey apologized to the team, and they played the sound bite all day with him saying "sorry." The coaches and offensive line are terrible. Joey had no time to throw, and when he did, he had trouble. When the game was on the line, they failed: "This team doesn't believe it can win." I heard Dan Miller call the last play that went incomplete

125

and ended the game—the same depressed voice we heard from Mark Champion for years, without the "holy mackerel." What is really amazing is that the Lions are two plays away from being 4-1 this year instead of 2-3. The soap opera continues next week in Cleveland for our first-place Lions. The North division is 0-9 on the road this year.

There were two interesting statistics that tell you everything you need to know about this past game. The Lions offense had a negative two yards on their last 10 plays of the game, and the defense, which had given up only four first downs to Carolina through three quarters, gave up 10 fourth quarter first downs. The talk about Harrington will not stop. He will probably play his last game as a starter this weekend in Cleveland. Good luck, Joey!

A quote from Harrington in the paper: "They will not bring me down." I have to give him credit—he seems to take all the hatred from fans and negative comments from the media and other players, and keeps going forward. He is very well thought of, a nice guy. I guess when you have been paid $25 million for five years, it can toughen you up. Garcia is getting half of the reps in practice this week—he will clearly get his chance in the next few weeks. The Lions soap opera continues!

It is John Joseph Harrington's 27th birthday today. What a present he might receive from his boss—being benched in favor of Jeff Garcia. We should probably call him J.J. instead of Joey. The only thing you can predict about the Lions is that, in the end, it will be bad! Fans can't wait for the soap opera to continue Sunday in Cleveland.

Joy in Lions' town! Detroit beats Cleveland 13-10 to go to 3-3 and stay in first place tied with Chicago. Mariucci makes the switch to Garcia, and he played great. He ran for a touchdown, completed about 66 percent of his passes, throwing for 210 yards with no interceptions. And the key was making the big play at the right time. It looked totally different than Harrington. I think Joey can see the writing on the wall; he won't get back in this year unless Garcia gets hurt.

The bad news was that the Lions had three severe injuries to key players. With the Lions, you learn early that you cannot have good news without some bad thrown in. A key receiver tore his Achilles and is out for the year. Our two best defensive players were also hurt—Shaun Rogers with a knee that could keep him out for the year or at least a month; and Dre' Bly, our top corner, who dislocated his wrist by running into his own man. It was Bly who was covering Charles Rogers in practice the first time he broke his collar bone two years ago. Hard to say how long he will be out or if surgery will be necessary. This has got to give the team a big lift, watching a guy who had the leadership and the skills to give them a chance. With Joey, it was like we had no offense.

On October 30th, 2005, the Bears beat the Lions 19-13 in overtime on an interception returned for a touchdown thrown by Jeff Garcia. It's Halloween day and the radio sports shows are playing the sounds of people screaming and shrieking when the Lions offense is mentioned. I went to the game instead of golfing on one of the last beautiful days in the Detroit area (67 degrees); a bad choice. My good buddy offered me a free ticket down near the field. Just before the last play of the game, my friend says to me, "I can't watch this anymore," referring to the Lions' defense. He suggested it as the new title to this book.

The final statistics were better than I thought. Garcia was 23-35 for 197 yards. We must have run for 100 yards. The offense is so boring that it really is hard to watch. The defense is playing well, giving up only 19 points. You should win a game when the defense allows 19 points. Garcia was rushed and blitzed constantly, never having more than two seconds to throw the ball. Our offensive line is the biggest problem on the team without question. We were also frustrated by our defense never blitzing. Our coordinator doesn't believe in it. It was a Bears blitz that won the game for them when the Lions were on the Bears' 37-yard line with two minutes left in regulation. Garcia was sacked at the 45-yard line, taking them out of field goal range.

Mariucci has the same depressing speech after the game. He refuses to change the offense, refuses to direct the defensive coordinator to blitz occasionally, and has not been able to put together an effective offensive line. I think we should take another receiver in the first round next year! I do not think he is a very effective coach. He is now 14-25 as the head coach of the Lions. And Millen is now 19-52 as the president of the team in four and a half years. I'm starting to get to the point I did last year when I was rooting for the Lions to lose. Of course, they won that game against Arizona. They happen to play Arizona two weeks from now. Will I root against them again? I think I need to see my therapist. The Lions illness is returning and I find myself dazed and confused.

The sports talk shows say it's "Groundhog Day all over again." The Vikings win 27-14 over the Lions. This one was over when the Vikings scored 21 points in just over three minutes of the second quarter. Joey helped them out, of course, with a fumble and an interception deep in Lions territory on consecutive possessions. Even though Harrington threw for almost 300 yards and completed 60 percent of his passes, he continued to look lost and ineffective.

Mariucci left Charles Rogers home for the game after returning from a four-week drug suspension. They said he was rusty from the layoff and did not have a good week of practice. I find it amazing that they bring a guy from the taxi squad to the game and leave home the guy who was drafted second overall four years ago. Rogers must have really pissed off his coach.

The wheels are starting to come off. You can see this season slipping away. If Garcia can return and be effective the rest of the way, I could see them winning four or five of their final eight games. If he is not effective, they will be lucky to win three more. I don't understand playing Harrington yesterday. After benching him for Garcia two weeks ago, and all but saying his career was over in Detroit, they put him back in. It was obvious the Lions had no chance of winning that game with Harrington as quarterback. Why they did not start the rookie Orlovsky makes no sense to me. What's the worst he could do, lose? He might have given them a chance to win. With Harrington we had no chance.

They showed Matt Millen watching the game from a private box. He looked disgusted and ready to kill someone. I think he sees the writing on the wall. He is going to have to fire Mariucci if things don't change in the next two months. The only question is, do you keep Harrington under a new coach or let him go, too? How Millen has kept his job is beyond me. Chuck Schmidt, who was general manager before Millen, must be getting some quiet satisfaction out of this.

Watching the game was an interesting experience for me. I began watching with no hope of winning this game. It was actually a relief. No disappointment about the end result—I totally expected it. This was against a Vikings team that has been a laughingstock in the League to this point, and one that just lost their quarterback for the season to a knee injury. It is strange watching your team as a casual observer, but it is my professional obligation in order to finish this book. Throughout most of the second half, I was turning to the PGA golf tournament to see if Tiger would win another one. The Lions are so predictable, so bad, and so boring; my friend said it all the week before, "I can't watch this anymore."

Roy Williams said he was supposed to play 20 to 30 plays in this game. Was it poor communication between him and his coach, or a message from Mariucci to Williams? Mariucci supposedly asked Roy if he could go in when Mike Williams was injured, and he said no. I don't think Mariucci liked that. He is trying to send a message to his young, spoiled receivers who have performed far under their expectations.

A radio show this week said that Bill Ford Sr. will not get rid of Millen—he likes him too much, and that is more important than winning. The host called for Millen to do the honorable thing and resign after the season. Although I see his point, it's a little hard to walk away from a job that pays you five million dollars a year. As Darryl Rogers once said, "What's a guy got to do around here to get fired?"

The Lions are at home this week against Arizona. If they lose this game, the wheels have officially come off and the season is over. We don't know if Garcia is healthy enough to play. It makes no sense to play Harrington. I hope they consider the rookie Orlovsky. They play at Dallas the next week, and home to Atlanta on Thanksgiving Day. I don't see them having much of a chance to win either of those, so they could be 4-7 at that point if they beat Arizona.

Many of my friends and I are not renewing our season tickets. What is the point? We have to accept that this is going to be a losing franchise until the Fords no longer own the team. Since he bought the team in 1964, the Lions have had 14 winning seasons and 34 losing seasons since 1964—no wonder Lions fans are discouraged and struggling with mental illness from September through December each year! And after the NFL season, we get to look forward to a long, cold winter. Thank God for the Red Wings and Pistons.

The Lions beat Arizona in the ninth game, 29-21 to go to 4-5. I even bet that we would cover the four-point spread. Harrington was very good, throwing for three TDs and zero interceptions. His QB rating was close to 120. Roy Williams, who is by far our best receiver, caught all three TDs. We had a good running game as well. There is only one problem with this win. It was against one of the worst teams in the NFL; Arizona had the ball with one minute to go with a chance to tie!

The reason I am not excited about this win is that I had given up on the season weeks ago. I looked at the Lions record to this point after nine games. Their four wins have come against teams with a combined record of 9-27; their five losses are against teams with a combined record of 28-16. Does that explain why they have no chance this year?

They are playing at Dallas next week; no chance. Home for Thanksgiving against Atlanta, a 30 percent chance of winning. Home against Minnesota, 50 percent chance; at Green Bay, a 30 percent chance. Home to Cincinnati, a 20 percent chance; at New Orleans, a 50 percent chance. Their last game is at

Pittsburgh—no chance. They will win two or three more games and end up either 6-10 or 7-9. The Bears have won five in a row and will win the division with at least nine wins. It is very possible the Lions will win only one more game and end at 5-11. Their final record has a lot to do with if Garcia is healthy enough to play; with him, I say they win three more—if it's Harrington, I say they win one more.

Seven games left in the season. Hope is all but gone. Why are Lions fans so dumb when it comes to their team? History has shown us that we are not very good. We are envious of other cities with great NFL teams: New England, Denver, San Francisco, Dallas, Green Bay, New York, Indianapolis, and Washington. All are teams that have won championships over the past 20 years. I believe Indianapolis will win this year.

The wheels are about to come off; there is no chance they will win both of their next two games. There is a 30 percent chance they will win one of the two. I believe they will lose both and go to 4-7. Watch all hell break loose if that happens. I hope I am wrong.

Dallas 20-7 over Detroit. The Lions get 18 penalties—the most since 1970. The penalties result in nine Dallas first downs—the second most in NFL history. I found myself rooting for five more penalties so they could set the all-time record. Actually, the refs made several questionable calls against Detroit. One of the penalties actually saved Detroit a touchdown, when Dallas picked off a Harrington pass and returned it for a TD. We were flagged for illegal procedure. The defense played hard considering half of the starters were out. Harrington looked decent, throwing down field several times. Roy Williams and Charles Rogers also looked good. But once again, we will have to wait until next year for the playoffs. The Bears are now 7-3, having won their last six in a row. Detroit is 4-6 and is four games behind Chicago with six left to play.

So, another year wasted. It will be interesting to see what changes are made; the most obvious one needed is a new coach. They may get rid of Charles Rogers. I think it is worth seeing Harrington one more year under a new system. It seems the defense has some great potential next year. There needs to be work on the offensive line—I hope they use their first draft pick here. Will the Fords clean house again and say goodbye to Millen? I doubt it.

In doing research for this book, I discovered that the Lions have averaged only 6.6 wins per year since 1970. That puts them in 27th place out of 32 teams. Miami has the most wins since 1970, averaging 9.65 per year. Only New Orleans, Atlanta, Arizona, Tampa Bay, and Houston averaged fewer wins.

No wonder fans are having nervous breakdowns over this team at an all-time rate. Our average season is either 7-9 or 6-10. The four times we won 10 or more games since 1970 was due to one man: Barry Sanders.

Tomorrow is the big Thanksgiving game against Atlanta. The Falcons need to win to be 6-4. The Lions can officially end their season with a loss. They will either be 5-6 or 4-7 after tomorrow. The big drama is who will start at quarterback? I'm guessing it will be Garcia. I believe there will be some significant changes after this year.

The *Detroit Free Press* headline says it all: "Stuffed, Mashed, and Cranburied." For the third straight time on national television, the Lions disgrace themselves and the city; Atlanta 27-7. Speculation after the game was that Mariucci would be fired the next day. Nothing happened. There are reports that Jauron turned down the interim coach position the last five games. This team does not want to play for this coach. They quit on him a long time ago. You almost feel bad for Mariucci based on how depressed he looked after the game, but he is simply not a good coach. The $10 million payout of his last two years will help him over the depression. Fans don't have that kind of fallback. A classic moment in this game: after a Lions receiver misses a pass in the end zone, he picks up the ball and throws it at Roary, the mascot. Roary is lying on the ground when the ball hits him in the face. This is one of the most symbolic things I have seen representing the utter futility and frustration of this organization. The mascot takes one in the snout, from its own player! I wanted this picture for the front cover of the book, but I thought the Lions might not give me permission.

The last five games are important for next year. You want to see what these young players have. I don't know why Millen just doesn't finish the season as head coach until they pick someone after the season. With four wins, we are the 10th worst team in the NFL. We don't even have much of a chance for the top five picks in the draft, and this year the top five are loaded. We should probably pick an offensive lineman anyway, and not be seduced by the skill positions. Here we are, just after Thanksgiving, and we are already talking about the draft in April. Such is the fate of a Lions fan.

Dan Miller of Channel 2 Sports first reported that the Lions brass may fire Mariucci after the Atlanta game. The Lions denied all reports—business as usual. Why not admit your mistake and move on? Because it's the Lions! Miller is in a strange position, as he was hired by the Lions to replace Mark Champion for the play-by-play on radio. I wonder how the Lions feel about his report.

I just heard that Charlie Sanders of the Lions came out with a book about the team this week. Darn, he beat me to it! It will be interesting to see if the book is a recap of his career with the Lions, or if he is critical about the last 48 years. I will read it for research. I am not giving up on this book. It is written by a fan for the fans.

Mariucci is gone! Now we have to work on Millen. How the Fords let him keep his job is amazing. It could have to do with Mr. Ford adopting Matt as his new son. We should call him Matt Ford! There are rumors that, next year, Ford will come out with its newest model, the Millen. Millen has made three decisions on coaches over his five years here. He fired Gary Moeller (who would have been better than both the guys he hired), and he hired Mornhinweg and Mariucci. He clearly should not hire any other coaches whose last name begins with the letter "M." Too bad, because I would like to see them hire Mike Martz of the St. Louis Rams.

Dre' Bly then says that it is Harrington's fault that Mariucci was fired. He said that he has been a bad quarterback the entire time he has played for the Lions. This shows you the lack of professionalism and problems that exist on this team. If I were Harrington, I would punch him in the mouth in front of the team!

I am going to see them play Sunday against the Vikings. Will they play harder for Jauron? I think that they will. Olson will call the offensive plays; Tollner was demoted and several coaches were also fired. They could essentially end the Vikings playoff hopes with a win. It's now time for these players to step up, act like professionals, and earn their paychecks.

They just named Garcia as the starting quarterback. This surprises me and may be the official end of Harrington in

Detroit. You never know with the Lions. It could be they are starting Garcia because of the negative comments from Bly about Harrington. Garcia has maybe one or two years left in his career; he is certainly not a long-term solution.

What more can you say about this team? The sports radio stations have been talking non-stop Lions all week. I may be going to the game this weekend against the Vikings. I would have been more interested in going if Harrington was starting. It's my chance to spend some time with my good friend.

Of the 32 NFL teams, 25 have appeared in the Super Bowl. Of those 25, 17 have had a Super Bowl win. The four teams that have never been to the Super Bowl are Jacksonville, Cleveland, Houston, and Detroit. You can't really count Jacksonville, which has been in the League for only 10 years, and Houston, which has been in the League for four years.

CHAPTER 12

Mass Nervous Breakdown by Fans: Will We Recover?

AS I SAID EARLIER, THE LIONS HAVE AVERAGED 6.6 WINS per year since 1970, ranking them 27.

December 4th, 2005: The wheels are really coming off. A fan uprising at Ford Field. The Lions were terrible again, losing to the Vikings 21-16. They actually had a chance to win the game at the end, but a Garcia interception ended that. My buddy and I were so bored by the game that we left in the middle of the third quarter. Garcia was so awful and the offense was so boring, it was hard to watch.

Before the game, I was outside and saw security staff collecting paper bags from fans, telling them they were not allowed inside. The bags were to be put over their heads as a symbol of being embarrassed by the team. The guard had about 10 bags in his hand. That was the first sign of the day that we were about to enter a place that had rules similar to old Russia. Fans in the second half began holding up signs saying, "Fire Millen." One fan ran around the stadium with such a sign and was eventually tackled by security. He was told never to come back to Ford Field; this was all shown on Fox television. The bottom line is that the Fords don't like criticism.

When Millen fired Mariucci last week, he said he must see the potential of the younger players. So, what do the Lions do? They start a 35-year-old quarterback who will not be with the team next year and do not dress Charles Rogers. That makes a lot of sense! You don't dress a guy who was the second overall pick in the draft four years ago and who is the fastest guy on the team? He has to earn playing time in practice? The second overall pick doesn't *earn* playing time—he is out there, period. This decision shows that the Lions are getting rid of both Rogers and Harrington next year. I am happy for Harrington; he will probably be pretty good at starting over with an organization that knows what it's doing.

My buddy had a great idea for a fan protest at the last game in two weeks against the Bengals. When the game starts, all the fans in the lower bowl get up and go to the concessions for 10 minutes, leaving all the seats empty. The television broadcast would certainly show the empty seats and comment on the fans' frustration. I do believe that something noteworthy will take place at the last home game.

One of the sports radio stations is organizing an "angry man's march" outside Ford Field for the last game in two weeks. They are renting a billboard near the stadium to send a message to the Fords about the Lions. They will meet at one of the bars near the stadium and have asked fans to bring unused tickets to burn. This should be something to see. The message to Ford is that he owns the team, but the Lions belong to the fans of Detroit!

Angry fan week continues on the sports radio shows. Today, the theme is "adopt an NFL team." Vote for the Bengals, Colts, and Broncos have been called in. This team's many problems give these shows great material. I'm sure it's not very funny for the players, even though they make a lot of money. I really have no idea what it feels like to play at this level in a losing situation. At least NFL players pick up that big check to help lift their spirits; I'm guessing it may be harder for college football players who play for the love of the game, pride of representing their schools, and, of course, the women!

I heard that Red Wings fans were holding up "Fire Millen" signs at the hockey game last night. I don't think the Fords can do anything about that. I guess Red Wings management believe in free speech. The morning sports show was playing a game called "name that Millen debacle." It was when he said Mornhinweg was his guy on December 31st, 2002, and then fired him to hire Mariucci a few weeks later. I can't really blame Millen for that one; that happens all the time when a better coach comes along.

There was talk today, December 8th, 2005, on the sports radio show that Mike Shanahan has had a falling out with his owner and might be available. He might be a good choice for our new general manager, since he has won two Super Bowls. Maybe Millen offers him the head coaching job. A friend asked me the other day what I would do if I were the owner of the team. The truth is that I have no experience with football other than being a fan. The Fords have been owners for 42 years and Millen has been in football all of his life. They are supposed to know what they are doing. But I told my friend

I would try to hire away one of the top presidents in football. New England's, Pittsburgh's, Parcells from Dallas, Shanahan from Denver. We need someone with a proven track record. Millen had no track record. Mornhinweg had no track record; Mariucci had some track record but that was not enough. Who knows what to do with this God forsaken team? Help!

I picked up a copy of the *Detroit Free Press* in December of 2005. The headline read, "When Will the Pain End?" and it featured a photo of Bill Ford, Jr. I assumed it was an article about the Lions, but it was actually about the 60,000 jobs being cut in the auto industry, and the Big Three slipping to an almost 50 percent share of the auto market. I guess this is a little more serious than why the Lions are so bad. Football is just a game, but this had to do with peoples' jobs and feeding their families. We do get a little too serious about football sometimes, don't we?

Another *Detroit Free Press* story read, "Lions Fan Sells Loyalty on eBay." The ad on eBay read, "Former Detroit Lions supporter looking for new NFL team." The highest bid stands at $20 as of today. This fan is convinced that the Lions will never win until ownership is changed. Another article told the story of an ex-Lions player, Daryl Sanders, who quit the team in 1966 after three years with the organization. He was the starting left tackle at the time. The team went 4-9-1 that year and Daryl got a lucrative business offer and retired from football. He felt the Lions had "no vision" and felt they would never be a winner under the Ford ownership. This man knows how to see the future, doesn't he? He says that the organization is very dysfunctional now and always has been. There is no foundation and there never has been one. The title of the article was "Quitting Time" by Michael Rosenberg.

In Rosenberg's *Detroit Free Press* interview with Dick Stockton, who worked with Millen when he was a television analyst, the question was asked, "Did the fans get to Millen?" Stockton laughed so much, he could hardly speak. Then he said, "It doesn't mean a thing to Matt Millen. I'm not saying he doesn't care. He cares about the fans. He wants the franchise to do well."

It's nice to know that Millen is probably laughing at us, the fans, while he dines weekly with Mr. Ford to discuss the state of the Lions. Wouldn't you love to be at one of those dinners? The truth is that the fans are tired of Millen and Ford. We should have realized what Daryl Sanders came to accept in 1966.

The Lions will be on national television tomorrow night in Green Bay. It will be around 18 degrees. I saw three Lions players interviewed about the game and the first thing each of them said was how cold it was going to be. Isn't that amazing? You wonder why this team is considered soft and has a record of 4-8. I am guessing their thoughts should be about the game and the need to beat the Packers. The Lions are a six-point underdog going into this game. The Packers are 2-10! Detroit has not won at Lambeau Field since 1991. They have lost 13 straight games there, which ties them with Arizona for the longest losing streak in the NFL to one team.

The paper has an article today comparing the Lions to the L.A. Clippers of the NBA. The Clippers have been the joke of the League the last 25 years. They are finally good this year with a record of 13-5 presently. Elgin Baylor has been the general manager there for the past 20 seasons. In the media, Baylor thanked his owner for his faith and loyalty. The Clippers have been to the playoffs only three times; they have had 20 top 10 draft picks in that time. Baylor's record with the Clippers since 1986 is 522-1,022, with three playoff appearances. Millen since 2001 is 20-56 presently, with no playoff appearances. Will the Fords give their adopted son a chance to run the team for 20 years? It's possible!

The *Detroit Free Press* headlines read, "Night Clubbed," after Detroit loses to the Packers 16-13 on *Sunday Night Football*. At least the team didn't disgrace themselves. But it was really the same old thing. No passing game; Garcia threw a few good balls but was very ineffective. You knew it was going to be the same old thing when Detroit settled for two field goals inside the five-yard line in the first eight minutes of the game. Our inability to score a touchdown in the red zone is unbelievable. It is hard to score when you have no passing game. In the fourth quarter with the game tied 13-13, the Lions go for it on fourth and one.

I'm thinking, "Why not kick the field goal and take a three-point lead?"

Okay, they're 4-8, what's the difference if they go for it? After calling a timeout to discuss the play, they run a quarterback sneak with Jeff Garcia! Garcia is 6' 1" and weighs 188 pounds—he looked like a feather getting blown backwards. Joe Theismann said, "That's a horrible call."

They had just run two plays with our running backs to the right of center, which got stopped for no gain. The defensive lineman for Green Bay is about 365 pounds—one of the biggest guys you have ever seen—and they run right at him! Jauron is a terrible coach and has no chance of remaining with the team. I never liked his refusal to blitz when he was the defensive coordinator.

The play of the game was when it appeared the Lions had a safety after missing the touchdown on fourth down. They tackled the Packers running back in the end zone, but the guy threw the ball forward. They first called a safety and then reversed the call, saying it was not intentional grounding. What made it even worse was that the Packers were also called for holding, which would be another reason to call a safety. The refs decided the holding did not occur in the end zone, even though replays showed it did. The Green Bay coach went crazy, throwing a challenge flag. When the final decision was explained to Jauron, he accepted it like a sheep. No protest, no anger. We are the Lions; we accept things not going our way! Lions fans had "Fire Millen" signs in the crowd; one also said, "Don't Arrest Me," referring to the freedom of speech issue in "old communist Russia"—I mean Ford Field.

I was actually rooting for the Lions to lose, because the more controversy, the better my chances to finish this book and get it published. I actually shut the television off when the game went into overtime. I was up late the night before and was tired, but I also knew they would lose in overtime. I have never turned off a Lions game, let alone not watched overtime. What is happening to me? Is this a sign of health?

A local Detroiter runs a website for Lions fans and gets three million hits per month! That is unbelievable. He is calling for a protest at the last home game against Cincinnati. He wants all Lions fans to wear orange, the color of the Bengals. It will be an interesting game to watch on national television. The sports radio show today says the collapse of the Lions this year has been "an implosion of biblical proportion."

In *The Detroit Free Press* today, December 13th, 2005, there is an interesting article by Drew Sharp with the headline: "Curse Just One More Bad Excuse." Roy Williams is interviewed and asks, "Is this team cursed?"

He wasn't joking. He says, "I've never been on a team where things go wrong all the time, like, all the time."

Sharpe wrote: "Congratulations, Roy, you've officially become a Detroit Lion." He also wrote: "A dazed and confused Dick Jauron didn't have any answers during his news conference… Everybody has opinions on what's wrong, but I don't think that anybody knows… Find me the person that knows—that knows exactly what's wrong. Find me that person."

Sharpe also wrote: "Never before has the connection between the product and the consumer been as poisonous as it is now. Williams expects it to get ugly at the Lions' home finale Sunday against Cincinnati."

Roy Williams says, "It can't go on forever."

Sharpe asks, "Have you already forgotten what team you're talking about Roy? Who else but the Lions could have a safety reversed? Has that ever happened before in the NFL?"

He adds that the refs could have saved time in Green Bay "by just explaining that they were enacting the Lions' clause of the League rulebook, which says that any team incapable of helping itself doesn't warrant any assistance from the officials… Everybody wants this season to end as quickly as possible… It has taken two years, but Williams understands that the sins of the fathers become the burden of the sons."

The power rankings in the NFL show the Lions ranked 30th out of 32 teams. Only San Francisco and Houston are lower.

The statement for Detroit was that Roy Williams recognized that the team is jinxed, but thinks it might be different if not for poor management and underperforming players. It will be interesting at Ford Field on Sunday with protestors outside the stadium and fans wearing orange shirts. I do not believe this is meant as disrespect to the players as much as it represents the fans' anger toward Millen and the Fords. My buddy told me if this book had been finished, I could have sold 1,000 of them to people in the protest lines.

The Detroit Free Press had nothing on the fan revolt today. The *Detroit News*, however, had quite a bit written about the last home game this year, on Sunday, December 18th, 2005. There is a picture of Millen with his head in the target of a dart board with a dart in his forehead. It read "Aiming for Millen." There have been pictures of the Pope and Saddam Hussein holding "Fire Millen" signs. There is a feeling that what has really gotten the fans outraged was when security tackled the fan holding the "Fire Millen" sign at the last home game. Now, the Lions are saying they will allow signs at the last game if they do not obstruct other fans, or if they are not "offensive," whatever that means. At the last home game, the Lions found "Fire Millen" signs offensive.

The other picture of Millen shows him in a diaper with a Lions symbol on it, saying, "It's time for a change." That is funny. The message being that Millen has crapped himself and made a complete "mess" of the organization. They are organizing fans to wear orange. Dexter Jenkins of the Center for the Study of Sports in Society at Northeastern University in Boston is quoted as saying that fans in Philadelphia, Boston, and New York are "similarly frenetic over their teams." Jenkins believes that "the Lions fan revolt is a product of 21st century media," meaning the Internet and all the TV and radio sports stations available.

The concern the Lions' executives have, along with many fans, is that Sunday's game does not result in another black eye for the city of Detroit, especially since the Super Bowl is here in less than two months. What happened with the Pistons/Pacers brawl last year added to the already negative image of the city of Detroit. We will see what happens this Sunday.

A contest in the *Detroit Free Press* today asks fans to complete the phrase, "Yes, going to a Lions game can be extremely painful, but it's still better than..." I thought the funniest response was "...accidently being hit in the groin by a policeman's taser as I speak with an obnoxious telemarketer on my cell phone while watching a snow plow crush my car for which I dropped comprehensive coverage yesterday during a search for my lost puppy along a blizzard-choked freeway with no hat or gloves on my way home from being fired, but not by much."

Prior to the Cincinnati game, the *Detroit News* and *Free Press* headlines read, "Teed Off" with an article announcing that Lions jerseys are available reading "SUPER BOWLS" with a "0" underneath. Another one reads, "REBUILDING SINCE '57." Predictions of a pro-wrestling atmosphere are being made for Sunday's game. On a sports radio talk show, one caller said he would run naked onto the field! There is talk of a revolt. The billboard for the radio station 1130 will read, "Not this MILLENnium. Rebuilding since '57." Many fans were saying that they didn't care about the game anymore;

they wanted to see the side show—the circus of chaos. An article from the *Free Press* said that "if you want to make a statement to the Fords, stay away." And a sign at the last home game read, "Another Ford Recall."

A day before the last home game against the Bengals, headlines in the *Free Press* announces, "Lions Curious about Approaching Circus." One of the Lions players says he has never seen anything like this before: "We want to win as much as they want us to win... We are not going out there to lose... It's just disappointing that our fans are like that because, I'm telling you, one day we're going to turn this thing around and it's all going to be in the past."

I think we have heard that a few times in the past 48 years. Perhaps he is referring to "turning this thing around" by the year 2057—the 100-year anniversary of the Lions' last championship! I will be 102 years old—can I make it?

An interesting article by Drew Sharpe in the *Free Press* on December 17th has the headline: "Revolt Needs Dose of Apathy." He reviews a problem between the players after week three of this season when the Lions got a very bad call that cost them the game at Tampa Bay. Supposedly, on the flight back home, Marcus Pollard, a new member of the team this year but a veteran of the NFL, was upset about the team's mood of "indifference." This apathy from the players bothered him greatly and he let them know about it. He stressed the need for professionalism that defines a successful organization. The players basically told Pollard to go to hell! That he could "take his attitude somewhere else."

Sharpe writes: "It was obvious which direction this season was headed because apathy always trumps anger in sports."

Outrage by the fans represents an emotional connection to the team—"If you're mad, they've still got you. It's the uninterested that speaks loudest in the politics of sports management." Sharpe says, "If the players stopped caring, why shouldn't the fans?" He then goes on to describe the stages of grief as I did earlier in the book: denial, negotiation, anger, and acceptance. He states correctly that we are in the anger stage. My point earlier in the book was that because of the addictive qualities of football fans, we may never get to acceptance. The advice is to "ignore the Lions. Walk away. Close your hearts as well as your wallets. It worked in Cincinnati."

This is all correct in theory, but the problem lies in the power of the addiction. I propose the solution calls for all Lions fans to enter a 12-step program that we can call "Lions Anonymous." If you don't face the addiction, recovery is impossible! There will be no way to progress to the stage of acceptance and stay away. The "drug" keeps calling you.

The fans in Cincinnati finally stayed away and helped the organization to change. Now, after 14 years out of the playoffs (the longest streak in the NFL), they will clinch their first trip since 1991 against the Lions tomorrow.

Sharpe adds: "Lions fans think next time will be different. They will take another emotional shot to the gut, only to forgive once again... Walking in protest doesn't suggest a change in attitude. The fans are mad. Only when they're prepared to silently walk away would the Lions actually listen to the screams." A brilliant article by Drew Sharpe—one of the best written on the Lions this year.

The same day, a *Detroit News* article called "It's Going to Be Crazy" by Bob Wojnowski said, "The Lions should consider this to be tough love from the fans, like one of those family interventions when someone refuses to admit a problem."

He also wrote, "The NFL, with its parity-inducing salary cap, is set up for every team to get its turn. Almost every franchise has gotten a chance to sniff the top except the Lions." In the article, he quoted one player as saying, "It's not like the fans don't care... Oh, they care. But today, as they march and chant and plead, they might ask themselves another question, a question that should scare the Lions even more. Why should they still care?"

Wojo also wrote: "It was reported that the coach of the Vikings, Mike Tice, told his team to try to score early at Ford Field against the Lions, to make the fans turn on them. It worked! The Vikings' first offensive play was an 80-yard touchdown pass and the fans were on their way."

Cincinnati 41-17 over the Lions. Not as much chaos and anger as was expected. A few chants of "Fire Millen!" The "angry fan march" was peaceful and about 1,000 fans attended. About 15 percent of the fans at the game were wearing the Bengals orange color; five percent were probably from Cincinnati. Dre' Bly said that when he saw Lions fans with the visiting team colors on, it decreased his energy for the game and upset him. There is always an excuse for Lions players. He also said after the game that not enough of the players take this seriously. Now, that is rather accurate based on this season's performance. The great ex-Lion Chris Spielman said that wearing the visiting team colors was going too far and was in poor taste.

This one was great from the start; the opening kickoff is fumbled by McQuarters without a hard hit. It was a terrible performance by the team. The only bright spot was the play of Harrington and Rogers, both of whom will likely be gone after this year, although word has it that Millen has not given up on Harrington. One of the local reporters who covers the team said that Mariucci virtually ignored Harrington the two and a half years he was there. He never tried to work with him to make him better; he was supposed to be good at developing young quarterbacks. That is remarkable news if it is true. Chad Johnson caught a touchdown pass and instead of celebrating as he usually did, he looked confused and just handed the ball to the referee.

The *Detroit Free Press* headlines read, "No End in Sight" and "Home Groan." Fans wore "Fire Millen" bags over their heads. Posters of the Three Stooges, Bozo the Clown, and Millen were seen. One fan in the stadium had a blue headband over his eyes saying, "Lion Vision." Media reported about how fans appeared disconnected, sometimes booed, and had zero energy—even for sarcasm—to liven up the stadium. The radio host who organized the march said, "It's about loving the Lions—we deserve better." A soldier wrote on his shirt: "I joined the Marines to defend your right to watch this crap." Roy Williams said he felt the fans wanted the team to lose. A sign read, "Ownership since 1963: One Playoff Win... Mr. Ford: Who's the Real Problem?" "It's sad because it never gets answered."

Mitch Albom wrote in his *Detroit Free Press* column: "It wasn't the noise; it was the silence . . . There goes another year . . . Thank God it was the last home game; there's plenty of time to air out Ford Field before Super Bowl XL rolls around in February."

Rosenberg also wrote in the *Free Press* that, "It's not about bad football. That's nothing new. It's not even about historically bad football. It's about an organization that shows no signs of hope—and no stomach for the fundamental change necessary to compete for a championship. They protest because they care. And they think the owner doesn't." This is very well stated.

Things have quieted down quite a bit on the sports radio stations and the newspapers. No more jokes. Like, what do the Lions and Billy Graham have in common? They can both get 70,000 people to say "Jesus Christ" at the same time. One joke describes a young boy in court before a judge. The boy has been abused and beaten by most people in his family, so the judge asks him who he wants to live with. The boy says, "The Detroit Lions, because they can't beat anyone."

Harrington will start in New Orleans this weekend. Charles Rogers will be active for the game. This makes way too much sense! Who made this decision? Is Harrington being evaluated by Millen to see if he will be brought back next year? Or, is he playing in front of the Saints because there are reports that New Orleans is interested in Joey and have decided to let their QB Brooks go after the season is over? We will find out. Much of the current discussion is about the draft next spring. Most people feel we should pick an offensive lineman—there is a huge guy coming out of Virginia who is highly rated. This is all that is left for the woeful Lions fan in December—the draft next spring.

What else can you say about the Lions that hasn't already been said? Not much. I believe what happened in Detroit over the past month represented the first mass nervous breakdown by fans in sports history. We are in serious need of therapy, and lots of it! Am I the person for the job? I have a Master's degree in social work and significant experience with emotional and mental health problems. But am I ready to help fans cope with the grief, frustration, and anger over this team? It's a major undertaking. Should I see people individually or in groups? Perhaps I should see three and four generations of families at the same time, since this affliction affects people as young as 13 and all the way past 60.

An article in the *Free Press* reported that Jeff Garcia was so upset about his and the team's performance that he was "in tears, or close to tears." This is what the Lions can do to a veteran who has appeared in three pro bowl games—bring him to tears! "What chance does a rookie have?" says Rosenberg, referring to Dan Orlovsky. Orlovsky is quoted in Michael Rosenberg's article, saying, "I want to be the quarterback of this team when they go to the Super Bowl." Isn't that a sweet thought? You can tell he is a rookie—give him a couple years for the realities of the Lions to sink in.

The article's headline read, "They've Suffered Enough." It was about the two players who have been Lions the longest: Jason Hanson for 13 years and Cory Schlesinger for 11 years. "You hope you can make it through another week, after another loss, at the end of another losing season," said Hanson. "You talk to friends. You talk to family. It's not a good time to be a Lion."

Schlesinger said, "The fans are great, they love football, they love the Detroit Lions, that's why I love playing here." Even though he "did not care for the fans' reaction" recently, he realized it is the players who need to look at themselves.

It would be very interesting to interview one of the players for this book. They are people trying to make a living for themselves and their families. I wonder how many players are really bothered by the losing, or accept that the Lions organization is not going to produce a winner, and are grateful for a good job with a high income. I don't think a current player would be interested in being interviewed for this book because it is largely negative about the organization. Perhaps an ex-Lion who has no further relationship with the team?

The Lions just beat the Saints 13-12 on a last-second field goal by Hanson. It was very strange watching this. I was upset that they won the game. Why? Was it because I wanted that higher draft choice? Was it because a loss would be good material for my book? Or was it that I am sick of this organization and wish them only bad?

I told my daughter that I had to drop her off at her grandparents' at 12:30 p.m. instead of 2:00 p.m. because the Lions started at 1:00 p.m. NFL fans are so ingrained to be in front of their TV sets for the game that Sundays are planned around the start time. I asked myself, based on how terrible this season has been, why do I care about getting home by 1:00 p.m.? It's because we have done it all our lives—it's hard not to watch or ignore the magic of NFL football. I also needed to watch it in order to complete this book and witness for myself the final moments of the 2005 season. I began writing this book one year ago after the Lions missed the extra point against the Vikings. So much has happened since.

The final few minutes of the Saints game was interesting. Roy Williams had dropped several balls during the game. The statistic shown was that Detroit and New Orleans led the

NFL in dropped passes with 36 and 37 each, respectively. The Lions had about 12 penalties in this one, with five false starts. I was starting to say goodbye to Harrington as the game wound down. I was actually rooting for him at the start of the game. He led the team 75 yards down the field the first drive, looking excellent, and then throws a horrible pass to Roy Williams in the end zone for an interception. He then gained only 55 yards during the second and third quarters. I felt that Harrington still might be very good in the NFL, but by the end of the game, I was again wanting him out of Detroit. This would be for Joey's sake and for the Lions. After Harrington fumbled the third down snap and looked ridiculous, it was fourth down and 17. I was waving goodbye to another game lost and goodbye to Harrington. He then throws a pass to Roy Williams, who makes a great catch, out-jumping the defender for a 50-yard gain to the Saints' 35-yard line. Usually, I would be very excited. But I was pissed off that they made the play. Harrington hits Roy Williams for another completion; with no timeouts, the field goal team runs out on the field. Why not spike the ball so the field goal team doesn't have to rush? It reminded me of the play earlier this year in college football when the Spartans did the same thing at the end of the half against Ohio State. They blocked the field goal and ran it back for a touchdown. The Lions executed the field goal perfectly (don't get to say that very often) and win the game as the clock runs out. Shaun Rogers' TD on a fumble recovery was an amazing play, as he dragged three Saints 10 yards into the end zone. He is a special athlete and is going to the pro bowl. The Lions won this one without an offensive touchdown. We are playing the Steelers in the last game. Pittsburgh needs a win to make the playoffs.

What do you think the result of this one will be?

A *Detroit Free Press* headline read, "Hanson Unfazed by Confusion" above an article saying that, "There was confusion on the sideline." Has this ever happened before? If that field goal would have failed, all we would have been talking about was why they didn't spike the ball after the first down. I heard the winning field goal called by Fox 2 Sports Anchor Dan Miller on the radio; he sounded as though the Lions had just won the Super Bowl, declaring that the Lions won and wishing everyone a Merry Christmas. It was sort of sad. We have to get excited about beating one of the worst three teams in the NFL by the skin of our teeth.

A song has come out about the Lions on Lionbacker.com; I heard it on the radio this week. It sounded like it was making fun of the team, of course. The name of the song is, "It's the Lions I'll Buy," and it's sung to the tune of the 1971 song, "American Pie" by Don McClean.

The Lions fight song is "Gridiron Heroes." The lyrics are: "Forward down the field, a charging team that will not yield. And when the blue and silver wave, stand and cheer the brave. Rah. Rah. Rah. Go hard, win the game. With honor you will keep your fame. Down the field and gain, a Lion victory!"

The song should read: "Backward down the field, a doubting team that always yields. And when the blue and silver wave, close your eyes and pray. Rah. Rah. Rah. Go soft, lose the game. With shame you will keep your name. Retreat the field and gain, another Lions loss!" I am calling it "Gridiron Zeroes."

Here is an amazing statistic that says it all about the Lions' offense this year. Through 15 games, they are next to last in the NFL in TD passes with nine. Only the 49'ers have fewer, with seven. You cannot win a lot of games with so few touchdown passes. The sports radio show today with Terry Foster talked about how the number of telephone calls into the show were 4:1 about the Lions vs. the Pistons. We have the 5-10 Lions vs. the 22-3 Pistons, a team that has appeared in five NBA Finals in 17 years and has won three of the five. The Pistons are a team that lost both finals in game seven in dramatic fashion. They are a team that is off to the second greatest start of an NBA season in the history of the League. When I called into the show, my point was that the fans are not so much addicted to the Lions as they are to the NFL game. The Lions are all we have.

Listening to sports radio today, it is clear the "Lions illness" is starting to affect the hosts. Tony Ortiz and Terry Foster almost get into a fight over the Lions. Terry was upset that Tony said that the media has fueled the fire regarding the expectations for the Lions this year. Terry felt it was the Lions that fueled the fire and reporters only passed that onto fans. When I called in to comment on the rift, the producer told me they were only taking calls on the Pistons. The Lions debate went on another hour.

One of the funny aspects of this show on December 27th, 2005, was when Foster said that the Super Bowl for Lions fans is draft day in April. "The Lions should draft a Saint Bernard and they could sell it to their fans. The dog is really fast and will put us over the top!" Or they could draft a Smurf or a Pepsi machine and they would find a way to spin it to the fans. Are we that stupid? I think we are.

The picture in the *Free Press* of Garcia and Harrington with backs to each other, looking depressed, says it all. Under the headline, "Worst Season Ever," the article by Steve Schrader says, "We learned long ago not to ask, can it get any worse than this? Because that's like daring the Lions to show it can. Sure, they have had worse records, but with them imploding and the fans revolting, there are reasons to call 2005 their worst season ever." The article ends by saying, "But at least [the fans] are still coming to the games."

The *Free Press* on December 12th, 2005 has a headline: "Steely Determination Awaits Lowly Lions." The article by Nicholas Cotsonika says, "As Dick Jauron spoke, thunder rolled and rain beat down on the roof of the Lions' indoor practice facility. The team headquarters, intended to be open and airy, was dim and gray. It set the appropriate mood. This has been a stormy, gloomy season for the Lions, and it won't end until they weather one more game, Sunday at Pittsburgh.. The Lions continue to talk about playing for pride, being professional, auditioning for their futures, that sort of thing. None seem motivated to reach six victories."

What a surprise that none of the players this reporter talked to "seem motivated." They haven't been motivated all year. Is it because they aren't being paid enough?

I was talking to my good friend Chuck recently about football and the Lions. Chuck played college football in division three as a half back and coached high school football for 20 years, 10 as an assistant and 10 as a head coach. He felt the key to turning the Lions around was changing the attitude in the organization and with the fan base, that these are "the same old Lions." He feels that starts with the owner and filters down. He believes the importance of the head coach is overrated. He doesn't believe this attitude can change as long as W.C. Ford owns the team. He talked about owners like Jerry Jones of the Dallas Cowboys, Al Davis of the Oakland Raiders, Robert Kraft of the New England Patriots, and others who have been successful in breeding a successful, positive attitude. When Chuck goes to a Lions game, it is for the event. "It's about being with friends or family, going to Greektown or the casinos, and watching a little bit of the game." When he watches football at any level, he analyzes blocking schemes and formations to figure out what the coach is trying to do. He does this when he knows the team is very good. He does not do this when watching the Lions—it's "entertainment only."

Chuck feels most Lions fans don't really know the game of football. They got free tickets or are coming for a company function. When there are only 16 games, each game is magnified compared to other sports that play so many more. Why are the Lions so talked about? Chuck asked, "Why are soap operas so popular?" People love to see what is going to go wrong next, it's human nature. He feels the NFL game is so different, it's not just the skill or talent level—it's about the drive to be the best. Some pros get complacent; I get my money whether we are 2-14 or 14-2. The adrenaline rush that is critical may not be there for some players. NFL football is the most emotional game of any played. You get to focus on one team for a week; grown men cry after tough losses.

Although you have to have talent to win, you can hide less talented guys through your schemes. The chemistry that is critical takes years to develop in an organization. Sixty or more people working toward a common goal can be a very powerful experience for all involved. You have to have emotional bonds to each other. We talked about how close the Pistons are as teammates. A reporter last year during the finals couldn't believe that 11 of the players went out to dinner one night with each other. Chuck also talked about football being a game of sudden changes. You plan for a game and then injuries, turnovers, and strange plays can change those plans in an instant. It is a game of constant thinking on your feet. When discussing halftime adjustments, Chuck felt it was the players informing the coaches of what was happening that was the key. Chuck had a memorable season as the head coach of the Dearborn Pioneers in 1995. His team ended up 10-0; undefeated and with 10 straight shut outs! It was only the second time in high school history that has happened. ESPN ran a story on the team that year. Unfortunately, the team lost to the third-ranked team in the state of Michigan and did not make it to the championship game.

The sports talk shows are dying down a bit about the Lions. I think we are preparing for the relief that comes from having seven months away from the frustrations and disappointment of yet another lost season. A few comments included predictions of a 6-10 record next year and the hiring of the Lions' first Black head coach. There was some controversy over comments by Damien Woody that were reported. He said that if he knew about the problems in the Lions organization, he would have never come to Detroit. That kind of remark is just what the team needs in trying to bring other quality free agents here. He took a very high salary from Detroit and callers were questioning if he played well enough to earn it and say things like that. Once again, finger pointing, a lack of loyalty, and chaos. A lot of the players' comments the past month as the wheels fell off clearly depicted the problems of attitude, chemistry, and professionalism that have existed on the Lions for many years. Or has it been just a simple fact of not enough talent? I don't know anymore; I think I'm overloaded on this team and am looking forward to the break from the daily analysis.

This "Lions illness" can be so hard to figure out. I was telling my buddy the other day about my good friend who is thinking of giving up his two tickets on the 25-yard line, 17th row—very close to the field. After telling everyone I know that I was not renewing my terrible upper deck seats next year, my first reaction to my friend was, "No! Me and Larry will take them." What is it about this illness that gets such a grip on you? Is it that it is the only affordable season ticket of the four major sports due to how few games are played? Is it the NFL magic that has waiting lists of 5-10 years in some cities? I will figure it out someday.

December 31st, 2005: We say goodbye to another year. It was one of frustration for the Lions and their fans. The *Free Press* headlines read, "Lions in Limbo—Who Will Return?" and "Final Curtain?" and "Endgame for Joey, Jauron, and Rogers?" Drew Sharpe writes that Harrington "needs a fresh start... If that means forcing his way out of town, leaving the Lions with the suicidal task of finding both a number-one and -two quarterback in the off season through free agency or trades, then so be it. Turn the screws to 'em... If a player has the chance to orchestrate his exit out of this insane asylum, why wouldn't he?" He adds that, "Joey has always conducted himself cordially and professionally." I agree. Get out while you can, Joey!

The Lions' record at Pittsburgh is 0-5-1 since their last victory on November 13th, 1955. Let's see, I was two and a half weeks old when that last win took place in Pittsburgh! When you've waited a half century, what's a little more? I'm predicting a 31-3 halftime score. And the final score of 44-10.

What do I know. The Steelers lead 21-14 at half. Harrington looks fantastic throwing two TD passes and a QB rating of 146! But of course, the Lions are the Lions, and Eddie Drummond fumbles a punt leading to the go-ahead touchdown. Special teams allow an 81-yard TD on a punt return, and another return for 63 yards that Hanson saves. A fumble late in the half by the Lions almost leads to another score, but Pittsburgh throws an interception on the last play. It is the best the offense has looked all year, against the third ranked defense in the NFL. Jimmy Johnson says the Lions should keep Matt Millen and Dick Jauron for next year. Howie Long says the Lions are like a bad stock: up and down, up and down. I don't recall much up, do you? Terry Bradshaw makes hand motions like a fish flopping back and forth. We are so proud of our team.

I am listening to the start of the second half while I am working on this book. No need to watch it—I can hear the predictable TD drive quickly down the field by the Steelers: 28-14—it will get worse. Jerome Bettis gets his third TD of the day in his final home appearance. The Lions come back on Harrington's third TD pass of the day to Roy Williams. This is after Williams dropped an easy 20-yard pass earlier in the drive. Harrington and the offense look the best they have all season. The amazing statistic shown about Bill Cowher and the Steelers: They are 99-1-1 when leading a game by 11 points or more.

Pittsburgh scores again: 35-21 as the third quarter comes to an end. Fifteen minutes left of our Lions this year. Thank God! It's been a long, painful year for us fans. I'm sure it has been similar for the players, but at least they get paid to deal with this. Detroit gets an interception with seven minutes left. During the drive, a 20-yard pick up by Roy Williams is taken away because Kevin Jones is called for illegal procedure. Key mistakes at the worst times are a Lions trademark. Harrington is 2-9 since being on fire. Pittsburgh has had only two head coaches since 1969—amazing!

CHAPTER 13

Thank God the 2005 Season is Over!

THANK GOD THE SEASON IS OVER. FINAL SCORE, STEELERS 35-21. I thought it would have been much worse. You have to give the players and Jauron credit for playing hard and preparing for this one. I guess they do have professional pride as athletes. Jauron told the team to be prepared for the Steelers to try to crush them because of the playoff implications of the game. This game showed that the talent on the team is not as bad as their record. As the *Free Press* stated on January 2nd, 2006: "The Lions are suffocated by a losing mentality." The headline read: "Steelers Drop Curtain on Lions" and "Lost! Can Lowly Lions Be Rescued?"

Mike O'Hara wrote in his *Detroit News* column that, "The Lions have a national image of a franchise in disarray, with players who lack talent or underachieve—or both. 'We took a beating in the public eye,' said Damien Woody. 'It's a perception of you. You are guilty by association. You mention you play for the Detroit Lions—you're looked at like a villain.

It's not fair.' There are a lot of guys here who get it." O'Hara points out the five keys to fixing this organization: 1) Hire the right coach; 2) Settle on a quarterback and support him; 3) Fix the offense; 4) Change attitudes; and 5) Leadership.

Now what? No more waiting for Sunday at 1:00 p.m. anymore. I will watch the playoffs and the Super Bowl as a fan of the NFL, but it's nothing compared to watching your team in the post season. The healing can now begin for all of us once again. It will take two to four weeks for some of the bitterness to go away. Talk radio will continue its daily obsession with the Lions with talk of the new coach, the draft, the players coming back, and management. It won't die down until after the Super Bowl. From February through April is when the majority of the healing takes place. We are sucked back in for the draft. Then, as August approaches with the first preseason game, we will once again believe our Lions will make it this year. The seasons changing are like a re-birth of life and hope. From now until the next NFL season, the fans of Detroit are lucky enough to have the Red Wings and the Pistons. They will get us through the long, cold winter.

I love this football team we call the Detroit Lions. I love the city of Detroit. It's part of who I am as a person. I will continue to recover my mental health, but my addiction is a life-long problem. A relapse can occur at any time. I know I am getting healthier because I am committed to following through on giving up my season tickets.

The *Free Press* reviews the coaching candidates: Maurice Carthon from Cleveland, Tim Lewis of the Giants, Russ Grimm of the Steelers, Al Saunders of the Chiefs, Jim Schwartz of the Titans, and Mike Singletary of the 49'ers. *Detroit News* columnist Mike O'Hara feels Carthon would be the best choice because he comes from the "Bill Parcells training ground. Carthon has an intense, no-excuses work ethic that matches the personality of Lions president Matt Millen... Whomever Millen hired, the Powder Puff Spa is closed. Get ready to work, Lions."

The radio talk shows on the day after the season ended for Detroit is 100 percent Lions talk. Spindler and Caputo spent two straight hours talking about the coaches available after several more were fired, interviewing Jeff Garcia, and taking calls from fans. Little talk about the bowls, the college national championship in two days, or the 24-4 Pistons. This is what the disease can do to you.

The radio stations report that the win at New Orleans, giving them five for the season, cost them the number two pick overall. We could have had Matt Leinart from USC! We could have had the top offensive lineman from Virginia Tech. We will now pick ninth. Even when they win, the Lions get it wrong. Shawn Merriman from San Diego, a defensive end is going to the Pro Bowl. He was available when Detroit picked Mike Williams at number 10. It looks like another bad choice, doesn't it?

January 3rd, 2006: The *Detroit Free Press* headlines read "Now, We Wait" and "Season of Turning Points—All Downward." In articles by Nicholas Cotsonika, Damien Woody recalls the 21-20 loss to Carolina as a key game. The article said: "When your defense scores two touchdowns, causes four turnovers, and you still lose, that's bad. That's real bad. We couldn't do anything on offense. That might have been the worse offense I've ever seen."

Joey Harrington made another interesting statement to the *Free Press*: "I would go somewhere to be valued. If a head coach said to me, you know what? We think you're the best number two quarterback in this League, and we value you as that; that may be good enough for me."

This is a pretty amazing statement from Harrington. Most guys want the starting quarterback job only. Especially at 27-years-old! I guess the statement brings in the human factor that people need to be valued and wanted. He has felt very little of that in Detroit. I believe him when he says it will not be about money. Harrington has made almost $30 million in Detroit in four years. He is set for life with money. The article by Drew Sharpe said that Millen should come out from hiding and explain how he will go about his search for a head coach. Sharpe wrote: "Silence becomes arrogance, and Millen has remained silent since he fired Mariucci."

Drew Sharpe's article quoted Millen as saying that "the new coach's challenge would be to change the team's attitude. The one thing that doesn't exist right now for whatever reason is confidence and a belief, and those things can take talent and push it to a whole other level. You've seen it happen; I've seen it happen. We're watching it happen right now in the League in the playoffs. There are teams that are just okay, and they're playing pretty darn good because they think they're good. It makes a big difference."

Detroit Free Press headlines on January 4th, 2006 read: "Millen: I share your pain." Haven't we heard that before from a guy in the White House? "Millen's Plan C." The articles by Cotsonika said, "I didn't blame those people one bit. I was more ticked off than they were." Millen was referring to the anger by the fans. He added that Millen "breaks his silence and vows never to quit." He says, "To be honest with you, this hurt this year. It really, really bothered me." I sure hope it bothered him! He adds, "I didn't sleep very well; my hair turned white. This was the worst thing I ever went through... My blood pressure went through the roof."

Sharpe wrote that, "Millen, 47, didn't want to discuss whether he had offered to step down or if team owner William Clay Ford had given him a private vote of confidence. But clearly both have happened."

In the article, Millen said, "I mean this sincerely: I wouldn't trade positions with any GM in the League. And you want to know why? Because I believe what we have here is going to work. I believe that 100%, and I believe the people in this building believe that.... Maybe no one else believes in us. Maybe they don't. They don't have to. Only we have to believe it."

Wow, that is a rather confident thing to say. I have to give it to Millen; he has guts and he must be pretty tough to have survived this. Are you sure you don't want to trade places with the GM at New England?

The fan reaction to Millen's interview was amazing. The anger just won't go away. They will not give Millen a break. Maybe I'm just a sap, but his comments significantly increased my respect for him, and gave me some hope that this could turn around. Millen has been learning on the job, and I believe the learning curve may be turning. Fan comments on January 5th, 2006 from the *Free Press* included:

> *"Tell Millen to stop blowing smoke and get out of town. His only pain would be losing all that money."*

"I was more ticked off than you were!' Uh... no you weren't, Matt. Believe me, no you weren't."

"Millen could find a way to destroy the Colts."

"That was a heartwarming story about Mr. Millen. The only difference in our pain is $3 million and free beer instead of one that costs $7."

He is the biggest con man to come to town since Professor Harold Hill in Music Man."

Millen has done everything to convince me he's not the man to fix the Lions. He took over a 9-7 team and gave us the worst record in the NFL. Thanks to the Fords, we have another five years of his mess; give Matt another year. He promised to not draft anymore wide receivers in the first round. In fact, he is focusing on a quality long snapper from Rhode Island State as the Lions' first pick. Matt feels that if you are going to rebuild a team you must rebuild around the long snapper. This eliminates any further quarterback controversy; Millen hired Marty (the bar is high) Mornhinweg, a real clown. He followed with Steve (two yards, two yards, two yards, punt) Mariucci. Matt's track record indicates he will pick the most incompetent man for the job; wow, what a heart-wrenching story about a man with such compassion and drive. This leader has been definitely misunderstood by the public. He speaks of his new gray hair and the pain he has had to endure this year. Well, you should see my gray hair. I'm a season ticket holder and he is raking in the money. Fans have had to endure this pain since 1957; Millen says he wants the right guy with the right qualities for the Lions. What? Do fans care if the Lions fit Detroit? Matt, the fans care about WINNING and that's it! If that's his plan, then what he's really saying is that he has no idea, none, on what to do.

Writing this book has taught me several things. One, that I know nothing about the NFL or football in general, other than my opinion as a fan. Fans love to feel like they know more than the players, coaches, and administrators. It's all an ego thing. For instance, Rob Parker of the *Detroit News* wrote a column on January 5th, 2006, in which he ripped Millen apart. It was very sarcastic and demeaning to Millen and the Lions.

Parker wrote: "Hey, Millen, here's some advice, and it's free of charge. Now it's time for Millen to listen and take notes. It couldn't hurt to take some advice from a columnist who knows a little something about football. If Millen were in school, this would be considered cheating. After all, this column has given him all the answers to his most important test yet. Good luck, Millen. You'll need it." Parker's major advice was to hire Maurice Carthon as the new head coach and bring in Aaron Brooks as the quarterback. I can see why NFL teams get sick of fans and the media.

Saturday, January 7th, 2006: There is nothing in the *Free Press* about the Lions. It is the first time this had happened probably since May of 2005. Things are starting to die down. It's time to move on and start the healing process. When they select the new coach, things will start up again. Until then, heal, Lions fans, heal.

We are down to the final eight teams who have a chance to win Super Bowl XL in Detroit in less than a month. Here are the eight with previous Super Bowl appearances and wins: Indianapolis (2-1); New England (5-3); Pittsburgh (5-4); Denver (6-2); Carolina (1-0); Washington (5-3); Chicago (1-1); and Seattle (0-0). Only Seattle has never appeared in the big game, but their coach, Mike Holmgren, has won Super Bowls with the Packers. Their coaches are Tony Dungy, Bill Belichick, Bill Cowher, Mike Shanahan, John Fox, Joe Gibbs, Lovie Smith, and Holmgren. A rather solid group of coaches. Four of the eight have Super Bowl rings. What is their secret, and why won't they share it with the Lions?

I was listening to sports radio about a discussion on the Lions coaching search. Tom Kowalski said that the Lions are being very quiet about who is interviewing. They don't want the other NFL teams to find out and jump on the bandwagon and steal those coaches away. I thought how funny that sounded. You would think that other teams would stay away from anyone the Lions would be interested in, based on their track record.

The Sports Inferno radio talk show discussed the Lions coaching search. Word around the League was that Detroit was once again "the joke of the NFL" because they have targeted Russ Grimm as the next coach. Instead of seriously considering the coaches as they interview, word is they are token interviews to give the impression that they are doing it the right way. Millen supposedly wants Grimm, who he thinks is a tough guy who will instill discipline and motivation, but word is that when he did not get the jobs at Chicago or Cleveland last year, it was because of some shortcomings. It has been reported that he did not interview well; he comes to the interviews in very casual dress. He wore a sweat suit to the final interview for the Chicago Bears coaching position last year, which he lost to Lovie Smith. Also, he is reportedly not a very organized person. If this is true, there are serious questions about his professionalism and his administrative abilities. I'm guessing it might be important for a head coach in the NFL to have organizational skills. The other concern is that the Lions are the only team looking for a head coach that had a face-to-face interview with Grimm. The Packers had a telephone interview scheduled with him, but canceled when they selected a different guy. The Saints have had a telephone interview with him as well. Does that concern anyone else? I am feeling that they should get Haslett before the Bills sign him. But what do I know? The Lions have interviewed nine candidates by reports as of January 13th. We will see who the Lions select as their next leader. God help them!

We are down to the last four teams. The Steelers will play at Denver and the Panthers at Seattle. There was an amazing end to the Steelers/Colts game. Pittsburgh deserved to win the game, though, due to two very bad calls by the refs. The Jerome Bettis fumble was shocking and almost cost the Steelers the game. We root for Bettis since he is a Detroit native. It would be great if he could play his last game in Detroit for the title. I felt bad for Peyton Manning and Tony Dungy. The death of Dungy's son affected the entire team. But Pittsburgh and the Broncos were very smart defensively; they used many blitzes on Manning and Brady to change their flow. I never understood why the Lions have given opposing QBs all day to throw. But again, I am a fan—what do I know? I predict the Super Bowl will be Seattle against Denver. Since the Steelers are playing this week, Detroit cannot offer

Grimm the head coaching job. I hope they give it to Haslett.

The Lions are talking to Rod Marinelli today—a second interview for the defensive line coach of the Tampa Bay Bucs. He is in his late 50s, but has never been a head coach or a coordinator. Some people think he may be interviewing for a defensive coordinator position under Grimm. There is no way he could be the head coach, since his last name starts with an "M." Please, no more M's!

The word is that Jim Haslett will be named the Lions new coach by the end of the week. I feel it is a better choice than Russ Grimm of the Steelers. Haslett has been a head coach for five years, and before that was a defensive coordinator at Pittsburgh under Cowher. I would rather take my chances with an experienced guy vs. a guy who will learn on the job. We have seen the results from that strategy. Haslett was 10-6 with the Saints in 2000, but he has been at .500 since, except for last year with the Katrina mess. He was a linebacker for the Bills and has that tough guy look of a head coach. Some guy called in a sports radio show and said that if Haslett was hired as the next head coach, he would slice his wrists! I guess he sees it differently than I do. The truth is that no one knows who will be a great head coach. Only time will tell.

January 19th, 2006: We've got our man—Rod Marinelli, the defensive line coach and assistant head coach of the Tampa Bay Bucs. Another M&M combination, our fourth one. First it was Millen and Moeller, then Millen and Mornhinweg, then Millen and Mariucci, and now Millen and Marinelli. What are the odds of four straight coaches having a last name starting with "M"?

The *News* and *Free Press* headlines read, "Next . . . Lions Hire Who?" and "M & M Again!" The media will not stop the insults. Drew Sharpe wrote that he doesn't trust the hire, because it was made by "people who don't know what they're doing." I don't think today is the day to attack the Lions. I do believe they went about the search the right way and are trying their best to get this right. As I have said, fans and media don't really know what they are talking about for the most part. It is probably harder than it looks to run a professional sports organization. Millen was interviewed on the radio after announcing Marinelli as the new coach. He was obviously in a good mood and told a funny story. After arriving home from New Orleans at 1:00 a.m. with their 13-12 win, he walked into his house on Christmas Eve and saw a sign on top of the Christmas tree. It said, "Fire Millen." I guess his wife has a pretty good sense of humor. It has only been a few weeks since the end of the Lions' season, and you can tell that my anger is going away. I am starting to feel my mental health returning. Defending the Lions; aren't you impressed?

It will be very interesting to see who he brings in as his coordinators, what type of offense he decides to run and what he does about the quarterback situation. There is no question that our defense will be significantly improved. The talk shows should be non-stop about the Lions through the Super Bowl as Marinelli puts his staff together. Is there any chance I could be the team social worker?

I have to say that everything being said about this man is very impressive. I actually think that Millen may have gotten it right this time. He looks like a very tough-minded guy who will supply organization and energy into the team. With his cap on, he reminds me of Tom Landry from the Cowboys years ago. The sports reporter from Tampa said that he feels Detroit got the best coach of all the ones hired over these past few weeks. One of the Tampa Bay players called Marinelli the "best coach he has ever played for." Does Marinelli realize just what he has gotten into? It usually means the end of your career is close when you join the Lions. Good luck, Rod, you will need it.

The headlines about Marinelli continue for a few days: "This Lion Roars!" For the most part, fans feel he was a good choice, but there remains significant skepticism. There will be more Lions discussion as he puts together his staff. Today, on the two major talk radio stations, the subjects were the Tigers and baseball. The heat is finally off the Lions.

The Steelers will play the Seahawks in Super Bowl 50 in two weeks here in Detroit. These are two great teams and it is hard to pick a winner. I am leaning toward the Steelers in a close one. I am happy for the Seattle fans—they can now be taken off the list of teams that have never been to the Super Bowl. Are the Lions still on that list?

I just saw that Dick Jauron will be named the new head coach of the Buffalo Bills today. This has to be the first time a coach from the Lions has gone on to a head coaching job somewhere else in the NFL. I can only think of Don Shula going as an assistant with Detroit to the Miami Dolphins as their head coach in the 1960s. Usually, when you leave the Lions, your career in the NFL is over. I can see it now—the Bills go 12-4 next year and Jauron takes them to the Super Bowl, while Marinelli sucks and the Lions are 6-10 again. That might qualify for an "I Don't Believe It."

There is very little talk about the Lions at this point. The focus is clearly on Super Bowl XL. There will be more focus on the Lions once Marinelli names his staff and we get closer to draft day in April. The fans in Seattle went crazy when they earned their first trip to the big game. That is how I envision Lions fans if we ever get a chance at that moment. I am much more positive these days now that there are no games to play. I do believe I will see Detroit in the big game if I can make it to 90 years old. That gives them 32 seasons to get it right!

Donnie Henderson from the Jets has been named the defensive coordinator for Detroit. He worked under Herm Edwards, who is very well respected. The Bengals receivers' coach is said to be the front runner for the offensive coordinator position. It is very strange not hearing much about the Lions after a daily barrage for three months. I bet the players are enjoying their break—it couldn't have been much fun this past season, or these past five seasons! I heard that a reporter came out with a list of the top 10 worst executives in professional sports. Guess where Millen ended up? Right at number one!

I am using "Lions logic" to predict the winner of Super Bowl XL. The Lions played the Steelers tough the last day of the season. It was their best performance against a quality team this year. Because the Steelers struggled against Detroit, I am picking the Seahawks to win the big one. I will be rooting for Bettis and the Steelers, but Lions logic is foolproof.

January 30th, 2006: The radio talk shows are discussing the possible hire of Mike Martz as the Lions offensive coordinator. Mike Valenti of WXYT 1270, who is an outstanding radio host, also has a big ego and thinks he knows enough to be the president of the Lions. Everything out of his mouth about the Lions is negative. He has an amazing sense of humor and a way with words. Today he said that the Lions were "idiots" and you can't trust any decision they make. He said the "Lions make the Arizona Cardinals seem like the Vince Lombardi-led Green Bay Packers." He also said that Detroit had "an abortion of an offensive line." He is hoping the Lions pick the wide receiver's coach from the Bengals as the next offensive coordinator.

There are six days left until the Super Bowl. My numbers in my pool are terrible. I have Seattle 2 and Pittsburgh 9. Someone told me that the final score a few years ago was 32-29. I need a repeat. My buddy Woody, who is working the Super Bowl as the radio engineer, told me he might let me assist him at the Maxim party on Saturday night. I hear it is one of the biggest parties at the Super Bowl. Wouldn't that be amazing?

One month after the Lions' season ended, I can think more clearly about what this has all been about. I believe that all the passion, intensity, and anger over the Lions' failures represent our need for hope. Hope for our future. There has to be something to look forward to during the boredom of everyday life. The reason Lions fans have hope as August rolls around is because we need to believe in something; we need to look forward to something. Even though the reality of the past decades tells us that there is little chance of success, we believe this year can be different. Like my son Jason would tell me when he was a boy, "You never know, Dad." Everyone needs hope in life. When we say there is a chance this year, it has nothing to do with reality. It has to do with the human spirit that holds onto hope even when reality tells us otherwise.

The word is that Mike Martz will be named the Lions' offensive coordinator today. He will get a one-year contract worth two million dollars. If this is true, the Lions have themselves their best coaching staff in their history. It will be Marinelli, Henderson, and Martz. I think Millen has learned from his mistakes. The fans have got to be excited about this. All the talk will die down after the Super Bowl as we move towards the Red Wings playoffs in April and the Pistons playoffs in May. It will get hot again a few weeks before the NFL draft in April. Could this coaching staff be the turnaround that the Lions so desperately need?

The Steelers win 21-10 over the Seahawks. The headline read "XL-ENT." I thought it was a boring game, but Pittsburgh won because of three big plays. Ben Roethlisberger had a QB rating of 22—the lowest ever for a winning quarterback. He did hit a few big passes and ran very effectively. He was also the youngest QB to ever win the big game. Bettis gets the big win in his hometown and announces his retirement after the game. What a way to go out! Pittsburgh wins their fifth Super Bowl, tying them with the 49'ers and Dallas with the most wins. The NFL season is over. We will miss football until August. Detroit did a great job hosting the Super Bowl and improved its image greatly. I went to the Maxim party—what an amazing experience talking to athletes and Hollywood stars.

Jimmy Kimmel did his show live from Detroit and wrote a goodbye letter to the town on a full-page ad in the *Detroit Free Press*:

"To my new friends in Detroit, you did not have to be so friendly, you did not have to welcome us with open arms, you did not have to put extra chili on our Coney dogs, but you did. This is a great city, full of great people, and no matter what anyone ever says; you have nothing to be ashamed of (except maybe the Lions). On behalf of my co-workers, my family, and ABC, thank you for being so nice. You made us feel like one of your own and we won't ever forget it. I hope to come back soon. Your pals, Jimmy Kimmel and the crew of *Jimmy Kimmel Live*."

This was a very nice note about our city and respects the pride we have in the town where we grew up or where we live as adults. It's about who you are. Loving our football team is also about loving our city and our neighbors.

Of course, Kimmel couldn't just keep it genuine—he had to make the comment about the Lions. He is a comedian, so we shouldn't be surprised. That is the national perception, however—that our football team sucks. Until we change and become a winning organization, we will be the butt of jokes.

Another national writer for ESPN.com, David Fleming, listed Detroit's many problems, such as crime, poverty and racial conflict, and added the Lions to the list. He also listed the sports greats who have come out of Detroit, but rather than praise the Lions, he praised the fans for being the strongest fans in America. We probably are the toughest NFL fans in the country: Detroit, Cleveland, and Arizona. Fans from these cities better be tough to survive the many years of frustration our teams have given us.

The Lions signed Mike Martz to a three-year contract as their offensive coordinator. The three new coaches—

Marinelli, Martz, and Henderson—sound like a solid group of leaders. There is definitely reason for hope and optimism as there is every year. The way I will approach it next year as a fan will be to watch the Lions the first 10 games before I make any judgments or let myself become too attached to the team. They are going to have to show me things are different. I will not invest any money in the team at this point. The season tickets are gone. My hope is they can win six or seven of the first 10 games and have a shot at the playoffs. If so, the final six games could be very interesting, starting around Thanksgiving, when we play the Miami Dolphins. Good luck, gentlemen, you may need it. Most importantly, good luck to the players; it looks like things may be a little different around here regardless of the record.

The Harrington era is officially over. The Lions signed Jon Kitna and Josh McCown to compete for the starting position. They will either trade Harrington or cut him from the team. It was reported that there were some problems during a recent quarterback mini-camp with Harrington and the new coaching staff. They either didn't like his attitude and effort, or Joey told Millen that he changed his mind and didn't want to remain a Lion. We may never know. This may be best for both the Lions and Harrington, but it is clearly a blow to have to walk away from the third overall pick in the draft four years ago. In an article by Mitch Albom in the *Detroit Free Press* on May 15th, 2006, Joey described the moment he knew that he and Mariucci were in trouble. He came into Mariucci's office and told him that they needed to open up the offense. Albom wrote that Mariucci walked over to a sink, began brushing his teeth, and told Harrington he had interviews to conduct and to come back later if he wanted to discuss it. This tells you a great deal about the coach and problems on the team. It looks like Joey may end up with the Dolphins. See you on Thanksgiving!

It's April 29th, 2006: Super Bowl Day for Lions fans! It's the NFL draft. During a mock draft this week, Drew Sharpe of the *Free Press* picked Matt Leinart in the ninth position. Before he made the pick, he said that these college players are nice kids and have never done anything wrong, but they are about to hear the six dreaded words no college player wants to hear: "You are now a Detroit Lion." I thought this was hilarious.

Michael Rosenberg of the *Free Press* wrote that the Lions were looking for character players. That might leave Vince Young out since he "wore jeans to the White House and supposedly took one look at the Wonderlic Test and spent the next 30 minutes licking it... If Vince Young dropped to the ninth pick and the Lions pass on him, Young would inevitably develop into a combination of Michael Vick, Johnny Unitas, and Thomas Edison. This is precisely the kind of thing that happens to the Lions."

We select Ernie Sims out of Florida State with the ninth pick in the first round. He is an outside linebacker who is punishing towards the opponents. The only problem he presents is that he hits people so hard that he has had five concussions in his college career. The Lions said they have had him checked out medically and the doctors feel he will be fine. I can see it now: he is a great player for one or two seasons but has to retire because of head trauma. He sounds like a great young man who might provide emotion and leadership to the defense.

We selected a safety and a running back in the second and third rounds. We did get two offensive linemen in the late round, which may be a good move. The debate was that the Lions had both Matt Leinart and Jay Cutler available at their first pick but went for defensive help. I agree with the decision, but knowing the Lions' luck, or lack of it, you just know that one of them will become a star quarterback in the NFL.

May 5th, 2006: Stop the presses! One or more of the Lions players complained to the union that Marinelli had contact drills in practice, which violates the players' agreement.

"I Don't Believe It!"

I imagined the players telling their mommies that the coach was being mean to them. I could almost hear them saying, "He was making us hit each other, Mommy. Didn't you tell us never to do that? We miss our old coach. Coach Mariucci was nice; we had more fun with him. Maybe the union can get us back our nice coach."

I'm joking, guys; don't come after me now. I'm old and I break easily! A report on May 17th, 2006 identified three players who made the complaint: Shaun Rogers, James Hall, and Marcus Bell.

When I was telling my wife's sister about this, her three-month old son was on her lap. The baby had been fine for about an hour, but he began crying when he heard me say "Lions." The boy's name is Vance Spielman, no relation to Chris. Was this a coincidence or not? I think Chris Spielman would have been appalled by a player complaining about a hard practice.

This tells you a great deal about the previous head coach, the new coach, and the players. I guess you might consider the player who made the report "soft." I can't see anyone on the Steelers, Patriots, or Cowboys making this type of complaint. Their coaches would pull them by their ears and smash their heads into a wall. The team loses two days of practice time as a penalty. The players get two days off that are paid. Marinelli must be fuming! I'm guessing the player or players may not have a very good year with their coaches. If they are fringe players, they may be done in Detroit very soon. I would think the rest of the team is rather embarrassed by this. The Lions are already the laughingstock of the NFL; can you imagine the new jokes coming out of this incident?

A radio ad on May 23rd, 2006 trying to sell club-level seats at Ford Field for the Lions this year said the seats offer "the best sports experience in Detroit." A few weeks ago, the Lions came out with a statement in the newspaper that they "provide one of the best game day experiences in the NFL at Ford Field" and choose not to have cheerleaders for the team. An ex-cheerleader said that they should probably have a cheer squad so "at least someone would be cheering for them" It's amazing the Lions can even say these things publicly; I guess they might be true if winning football games is not important.

CHAPTER 14

Where Do We Go From Here?

AS I FINISH THIS BOOK, THIS LABOR OF LOVE, I HAVE DECIDED to end on a positive note. I was listening to the radio and heard Chris Spielman talk about the recent Super Bowl. He said that he cannot go to any Super Bowls because it kills him that he never played in one. His wife and kids went to one a few years ago, and he stayed at home. He also talked about how he still obsesses about what he could have done differently in the 1991 NFC championship game where the Lions got blown out by the Redskins. It hit me just what football means to this man.

The show concluded by saying that if the Lions fans could pick two of their players to play in a Super Bowl, it would be Barry Sanders and Chris Spielman. To know the quality of this man, you need look no further than Spielman as a husband. He took a year off from his NFL career when he was with Cleveland to care for his wife, who was being treated for breast cancer. We sometimes forget that players are human beings with problems like all of us. Spielman is one of the most inspiring athletes I have followed as a Detroit sports fan. He is up there with Gordie Howe, Steve Yzerman, Al Kaline, Barry Sanders, and Isaiah Thomas. Although Chris never got his NFL championship, he always had the heart of a champion.

My friend Woody, who has worked football games for years, told me a great story about Spielman recently. When people came into the Silverdome on Sunday mornings, Spielman would be there watching film at 9:30 a.m. This may not be that unusual, except that it was widely known that he usually watched film of his opponent all of Saturday night, falling asleep in the film room. When I heard this story, everything about why I wrote this book became clear. It's about passion for players and fans. It's about hard work and keeping the faith. It's about loving your team and your city.

The Detroit Lions hold a very special place in the hearts and minds of the fans and the city. We have been lucky enough to enjoy championships with six other teams; three pro and three college. But there is nothing like NFL football. We will continue to dream and hope that our Lions get this right someday. Until then, we will endure the tough seasons and torturous losses. Maybe, just maybe, someday we can watch our team in the big game. Maybe they will even win it. We will continue the cycle of hope, despair, and hope again, which is the cycle of life. I will always follow my team. Maybe no longer from my seat at Ford Field, but I will follow them, nonetheless. We will always love our Lions.

Cheers to the New Detroit Lions!

As this book goes to press, our Detroit Lions are roaring into the new season with a big win. And not just any win!

During the season opener on Thursday, September 7, 2023, the Lions defeated the Super Bowl Champions Kansas City Chiefs 21-20! For us lifelong Lions fans, this was the win we needed to boost our confidence and optimism that the Lions can actually get to the Super Bowl and win!

I hardly have words for this excitement, and I've written books about it!

So, as we look forward, let's look back to recap; the Lions finally put a cheerleading squad on the field in 2016. Lions fans, despite the current optimism, I know much of what I have written has been disheartening here, but don't give up the dream.

As the famous coach Jim Valvano once said, "Don't give up...don't ever give up."

We will see our boys turn this around; trust me, believe me!

APPENDIX A
Season Recaps: 1976-1980

September 26th, 1976: A botched extra point with seconds left in the game results in a 10-9 loss to who else but the Vikings. Sound familiar?

November 14th, 1976: The Lions lose to the New Orleans Saints 17-16, even though we outplayed them significantly. Total yards: Detroit 455; Saints 183. Landry throws for 310 yards, but three Lions fumbles, one resulting in a touchdown, costs them the game.

November 25th, 1976: Thanksgiving Day, O.J. Simpson runs for 273 yards, the record at the time. I was at that game to see a man who would later kill two people set this record. Oh, I forgot—he was found not guilty.

September 25th, 1977: The Lions lose to the Saints 23-19, even though they out-gain them 429-92 yards offensively. Isn't that hard to do? These are the kinds of performances that Lions fans scratch their heads over.

December 11th, 1977: The Lions pull off the "I don't believe it" play for once, beating Baltimore when Leonard Thompson blocks a punt for a touchdown with 14 seconds left, 13-10.

September 9th, 1979: The Lions rally from a 21-point fourth quarter deficit to tie the game 24-24 against Washington. The Redskins' kicker, Mark Moseley, misses a 46-yard field goal with eight seconds left in regulation. But you guessed it—the Lions are flagged for having 12 men on the field. Re-kick from 41 yards, it's good. Game over.

APPENDIX B
Season Recaps: 1981-1985

ONTO THE 1980S—THE BILLY SIMS ERA. WHAT A GREAT running back; next to Barry Sanders, clearly the best back in my lifetime. A tragedy that his career ended with a severe knee injury, against who else—the Vikings, of course. Sims debuts with a 100-yard plus game in a 41-20 win over the L.A. Rams. I remember watching that game and having a renewed sense of hope watching Sims run. After a 4-0 start, the Lions came out with their own, now infamous, version of the Queen song, "Another One Bites the Dust." Jimmy "Spiderman" Allen led the way. That was the end of their four-game streak, and the end of their season. To this day, that song is played after a particularly difficult loss. In game five that season, Atlanta beat us 43-28; the Falcons had two fumble returns for touchdowns and a blocked punt returned for a touchdown in the first half. The boys were probably a little tired from those nights in the recording studio. On to the famous ending on November 27th, 1980: the Bears win the shortest overtime game in NFL history when Dave Williams returns the OT kickoff 95 yards for a touchdown. Game over. This was after the Bears scored the tying touchdown as time ran out in regulation play.

Here are the other memorable moments from that era:

September 13th, 1981: The Lions lose the opener to San Diego, 28-23; the Chargers score a TD with 56 seconds left in the game. A rally falls short when the Lions are intercepted at the San Diego 1 yard line as time expires.

September 20th, 1981: Our friends from Minnesota beat us on a field goal with four seconds left, 26-24.

October 19th, 1981: On *Monday Night Football,* Eric Hipple has a career game throwing for four touchdowns as the Lions beat the Bears 48-17. It is the highest point total for the Lions since 1957.

December 20th, 1981: A dark day that Lions fans remember well, the Lions lose to Tampa Bay on the final game of the season, 20-17, costing them the Central title and a trip to the playoffs. Our Lions had three drives inside the Bucs' 20-yard line with no points, two interceptions and one on downs. "This team doesn't think it can win!"

September 19th, 1982: A new season, filled with hope. Sims runs for 119 yards and catches another 103 yards; he is only the 13th NFL player to do this in a 19-14 win over the Rams.

November 25th, 1982: A 57-day player strike is followed by another memorable game. Lawrence Taylor returns an interception 97 yards in the fourth quarter to beat the Lions 13-6. That must mean that the Lions were really close to scoring the go-ahead touchdown at the time—oops!

September 18th, 1983: Another new season full of hope; maybe this will be the year for our Lions. 10 key players are hampered by injuries. Sims breaks his hand during a 30-14 Atlanta win in game two. That can't be good.

November 20th, 1983: The Lions get their first ever overtime win, 23-20, over the Packers.

December 5th, 1983: The Lions beat Minnesota 13-2; take that, you bastards!

December 18th, 1983: The Lions beat Tampa 23-20, taking revenge for the heartbreaking loss from the year earlier and winning the Central division title. These were the good times with Monte Clark, when the Lions had a very good defense led by Doug English and Al Baker. On to the playoffs! This is getting exciting, don't you think?

December 31ˢᵗ, 1983: A day that will live in Lions infamy. The Lions out-gain San Francisco 412-291; Gary Danielson drives the team down to the SF 25-yard line after the 49'ers go ahead with 1:23 left in the game. The famous picture of our coach praying to the football gods as Eddie Murray approaches the 43-yard field goal attempt to go to the NFC Championship game. We all remember the results: the football gods said, "Hell, no. You must suffer once again. Happy New Year." Wide right, game over. Wait until next year. Remember that song "I Left My Torn-Out Heart in San Francisco"?

September 9ᵗʰ, 1984: On to a new season. The Lions beat the Falcons in overtime 27-24 on a 48-yard field goal by Eddie Murray. We could have used that in San Francisco nine months earlier! Timing is everything.

September 23ʳᵈ, 1984: Minnesota beats us in typical Viking fashion, 29-28. We don't even want to know the details, do we?

October 7ᵗʰ, 1984: The team has a memorable day when they lose to Denver 28-7 and have a record 10 turnovers (seven INTs and three fumbles). That's hard to do, even for our Lions, but they are known for doing the impossible and the improbable.

October 21ˢᵗ, 1984: Another day that will always be remembered by Lions fans: We beat the Vikings in Minnesota 16-14, but lose Billy Sims to a knee injury that will end his career. Of course, you would expect it to happen with the Vikings, wouldn't you?

November 4th, 1984: A 23-23 tie with the Eagles; the Lions pull ahead with an 18-yard field goal (doesn't that mean we were on the 3-yard line and almost had a chance at a touchdown?) with 63 second to go, but our defense couldn't stop the Eagles from driving down the field and kicking a 40-yard field goal to tie the game with three seconds left. Don't worry, there's still overtime to win, right? Eddie Murray hits the upright in OT from 21 yards and the game ends up in a tie! 21 yards! Isn't an NFL kicker supposed to make that? That means, of course, that the drive stalled at the 4-yard line. Darn, we were so close to a touchdown! I guess Murray never recovered from the 43-yard miss in San Francisco.

December 16th, 1984: The year ends with a unique performance by the Lions. They lose to the Bears as they sack the Lions 12 times. That's a lot of sacks— sounds like it should be an all-time record, doesn't it?

September 1985: The Darryl Rogers era begins. The coach who a few years later would have one of the most famous, gutsy quotes of all time: "What does a coach have to do around here to get fired?"

September 15th, 1985: Detroit beats Dallas 26-21, even though Dallas out gains us 554-200 yards but has five turnovers.

November 3rd, 1985: Vikings kick a field goal as time expires to win 16-13. What's new?

November 24th, 1985: Tampa wins 19-16 in overtime, after the Lions were leading 16-6 until late in the game.

December 15th, 1985: The Packers win by kicking a field goal as time expires. The Lions tied the game with 61 seconds left. Go, defense!

APPENDIX C

Season Recaps: 1986-1990

November 16th, 1986: The Lions beat the Eagles 13-11 and sack Cunningham 11 times. Wouldn't that have been fun to see?

November 23rd, 1986: The Chuck Long era begins. He sets an NFL record by throwing his first pass for a 34-yard touchdown. It would be the highlight of his career.

November 27th, 1986: A Thanksgiving game to remember. The Packers win the game by returning a punt 85 yards for a touchdown with 41 seconds left in the game. The Lions score 40 points—the most ever in a losing effort.

December 15th, 1986: The Bears win 16-13 on the final play of the game, kicking a 22-yard field goal.

September 17th, 1987: Another new season, hope again. Vikings 34-19; the Lions led at halftime 16-10.

September 20th, 1987: A players' strike with replacement players.

October 18th, 1987: The Seahawks win 37-14 in front of only 8,310 fans at the Silverdome.

October 25th, 1987: The day before my 32nd birthday, the Lions surely had something special planned for me. The Packers jump to a 24-0 lead, but the Lions come back to take a 33-31 lead with two minutes left. The Packers kick a 45-yard field goal to win the game 34-33. Of course, the Lions missed a 45-yard field goal of their own as time ran out. Happy birthday to me!

December 20th, 1987: The Vikings win 17-14 as Chuck Long throws an interception late in the game.

September 11ᵗʰ, 1988: The Rams beat the Lions 17-10; again, Detroit had a 10-3 lead at halftime.

September 18ᵗʰ, 1988: The Saints beat the Lions 22-14; a strange play in the game when the punter Jim Arnold for Detroit attempts a pass that goes incomplete from the Lions' 12-yard line. The receiver was not expecting the pass.

October 16ᵗʰ, 1988: The Giants win 30-10; again, the Lions were leading at the half, 10-7. Detroit had 113 yards of offense.

October 30ᵗʰ, 1988: The Giants beat the Lions 13-10 in overtime. Detroit fumbles the first snap of the overtime, leading to the winning field goal.

November 6ᵗʰ, 1988: Minnesota beats Detroit 44-17, out-gaining the Lions 553-89 yards.

November 13ᵗʰ, 1988: Darryl Rogers finally gets his answer to his question and is fired after Tampa beats the Lions 23-20 in overtime, with the Lions leading 20-17 with 52 seconds to play. A 52-yard field goal ties it and an overtime field goal wins it.

November 20ᵗʰ, 1988: Wayne Fontes takes over the team and leads the Lions to a 19-9 victory over the Packers. Little did Lions fans know then that Fontes would be the most successful coach we would have from 1957 to 2004.

November 24ᵗʰ, 1988: The honeymoon is over for Fontes. The Vikings welcome him as head coach by crushing the Lions 23-0. Detroit never crosses the 50-yard line! The 60 yards and 3 first downs are the third lowest production in team history.

December 11ᵗʰ, 1988: The Bears beat the Lions 13-12. Detroit goes up 12-10 on a late touchdown, but guess what? The Lions have the extra point blocked and Jim Harbaugh drives Chicago down for the winning field goal of 32 yards. Maybe the League could give the Lions a break and just award them an extra point when they get a touchdown. They just seem to have a way with extra points!

September 10th, 1989: A new year, a new player: Barry Sanders debuts and takes his first carry for 18 yards. He ends his first game with 71 yards in nine carries, but the Lions lose to the Cardinals 16-13 after a 33-yard field goal with 13 seconds left, wins it for the Cardinals. Get used to it, Barry!

September 17th, 1989: The Giants win 24-14 even though the Lions led at halftime 7-3.

October 8th, 1989: Minnesota wins 24-17 with three Lions interceptions, of which two are returned for touchdowns (15 and 90 yards).

October 15th, 1989: The Lions beat Tampa when Rodney Peete scores a touchdown with 23 seconds left in the game. Eddie Murray kicked the extra point to win the game. It's interesting that the extra point is mentioned in the game summary.

October 22nd, 1989: My birthday present from the Lions? A 20-7 loss to the Vikings; Detroit has five turnovers and are sacked eight times.

October 29th, 1989: The Packers beat Detroit 23-20 in overtime. The Lions fumble in Packers territory with less than a minute left in regulation, and then throw an interception on the first play in overtime. Sanders' outstanding performance of 180 yards on 30 carries is wasted.

November 5th, 1989: Houston wins 35-31; Detroit had a halftime lead, 17-14. Detroit threatens in the last minute, but throws an interception to end the game.

December 24th, 1989: Detroit beats Atlanta 31-24. We all remember this last game of the decade, as Barry Sanders rushes for 158 yards and three touchdowns, but refuses

Fontes and teammates, who urge him to return and win the rushing title. Sanders said the game was in hand, and the title didn't mean that much to him. I remember being disappointed when he did that. Lions fans don't often get to say one of their players is the best in the League.

September 9th, 1990: A new season, a new decade, a new result? Nope. Tampa wins 38-21. The Lions have six turnovers and are sacked six times.

September 23rd, 1990: Again, Tampa 23-20 on a last-minute touchdown.

September 30th, 1990: Green Bay 24-21 on a TD with less than a minute to play—a chance to tie ends when Eddie Murray misses a 44-yard field goal attempt.

October 7th, 1990: The Lions pull off a comeback after being down 20-10 at the half to Minnesota and win 34-27; we aren't used to the comeback victory.

October 28th, 1990: A great birthday present to me: the Lions beat the Saints 27-10, forcing eight turnovers. Shouldn't you score more than 27 when you get eight turnovers?

November 4th, 1990: The Redskins win 41-38 in overtime. Detroit led 35-14 in the third. Washington gains 674 yards.

November 11th, 1990: The Andre Ware era begins! Lions lose 17-7.

December 2nd, 1990: The Bears win 23-17 in overtime. Chicago kicks a field goal with 33 seconds left to force OT. Eddie Murray misses a 35- yard field goal in OT for the win.

December 16th, 1990: The Lions beat the Bears 38-21. Detroit has 411 yards of offense, the most in five years! Is it that hard to get over 400 yards?

December 22nd, 1990: A great and unusual comeback win for Detroit in -35 degrees wind chill at Green Bay. Detroit scores 14 in the fourth and bounces the Packers out of the playoffs.

December 30th, 1990: Seattle 30-10 over Detroit, but Barry Sanders wins the rushing title with 23 yards and beats out Thurman Thomas by seven yards (1,304).

APPENDIX D

Season Recaps: 1991-1995

September 15th, 1991: The best year the Lions will have since 1970. Detroit 17-13 over Miami; the Lions have a four-play goal line stance with under five minutes left in the game to stop Dan Marino from the 3-yard line for the win.

October 6th, 1991: Detroit beats the Vikings with three 4th quarter touchdowns, 24-20, as Sanders runs 15 yards for the winning score with 46 seconds left in the game. It's looking like a special season!

October 27th, 1991: A 34-10 win over Dallas. Peete injures his Achilles and is replaced by Erik Kramer.

November 3rd, 1991: The Bears win 20-10 in -8 degrees wind chill. Detroit was up 10-3 at halftime. The Lions are 2-13 on third down.

November 24th, 1991: Sanders runs for four touchdowns and gains 220 yards in a win over the Vikings.

December 8th, 1991: The Lions go 8-0 at home; their first undefeated home season since 1962, with a 34-20 win over the Jets. It is the fifth 10-win season in Lions history (that's all)!

December 15th, 1991: The Lions beat the Packers 21-17 in -18 wind chill. Mel Gray runs a punt back 78 yards for the winning touchdown in the fourth.

December 22nd, 1991: Buffalo scores a last-minute touchdown to force overtime, but the Lions' Eddie Murray wins it in OT with a 21-yard field goal, snapping the Bills' 17 home game winning streak. It is the first 12-win season in Lions history.

January 5th, 1992: On to the only playoff win I have witnessed in my lifetime! Detroit 38-6 over the Cowboys. Kramer is brilliant going 29-38 for 341 yards and three touchdowns. Herman Moore catches his first touchdown pass.

January 12th, 1992: On to the NFC championship game. We are one game away from the Super Bowl, could it be true? No! Washington 41-10. The dream is over. We were only down 17-10 at the half. It was a fantastic season though.

September 6th, 1992: Bears 27-24. The Lions take the lead on an 80-yard drive and touchdown with 1:12 left. A 74-yard drive by Harbaugh results in the winning touchdown with one second left! We were so close.

September 20th, 1992: Washington 13-10. The Lions miss a 49-yard field goal as time runs out.

September 27th, 1992: Tampa Bay 27-23. Mel Gray returns a kick 89 yards for a TD with 5:43 left. Bucs' 80-yard TD drive to re-take the lead. Lions go 79 yards in 42 seconds but fall short at the 3-yard line as time expires. Darn, we were so close again!

November 8th, 1992: Cowboys 37-3, the worst home loss for the Lions since 1964. Mel Gray sets a Lions record with eight kickoff returns. Does that mean the other team scored a lot?

November 15th, 1992: The Lions give the Steelers a scare but lose 17-14. Disaster strikes late in the fourth with the Lions up 14-10. Detroit fumbles deep in their own zone and it is returned to the Lions' 3-yard line to set up the winning touchdown. The game ends on the Steelers' 19-yard line after a great catch by Brett Perriman. Darn, we were so close again!

November 26th, 1992: Houston 24-21. The Oilers drive for the winning touchdown with less than three minutes left in the game. Is this fair?

December 20th, 1992: The Lions win 16-3 over the Bears. Ware throws for 290 yards; why didn't he ever make it?

September 12th, 1993: The Lions beat New England 19-16 in overtime. Drew Bledsoe throws a TD pass with 12 seconds left to tie it, but Jason Hanson wins it in OT with a 38-yard field goal.

September 19th, 1993: The Saints win 14-3; the Lions get three first downs and gain 29 yards in the second half. Is this why Ware never made it?

October 3rd, 1993: Tampa 27-10. Sanders runs for 107 yards in the first half; 23 in the second half (adjustments!). In the first drive of the game, the Lions go 80 yards on five plays. They looked like "world beaters."

October 17th, 1993: The Lions beat Seattle 30-10. Rookie QB Rick Mirer has problems (three INTs and three sacks); today he is a Lion!

October 24th, 1993: Happy 38th, birthday to me from the Lions. They beat the Rams 16-13, breaking an 11-game West Coast losing streak. This time, the Rams score a TD with 1:52 left, but miss the extra point (where did they learn how to do that?). Detroit kicks a winning FG as time runs out.

October 31st, 1993: The Lions have a come-from-behind win 30-27 after being down 27-13 after three quarters. Detroit scores with 40 seconds left for the victory.

November 7th, 1993: Detroit beats Tampa 23-0. Sanders runs for 187 yards; their 7-2 record is the best start for the Lions since 1962. Hard to believe that we have not been 7-2 in 31 years, isn't it?

November 25th, 1993: Bears 10-6. Sanders injures his knee. Detroit has four turnovers.

December 5ᵗʰ, 1993: Vikings 13-0. Detroit gets seven sacks and five interceptions.

December 19ᵗʰ, 1993: San Francisco 55-17. The 49'ers have no punts and gain 565 yards. They're pretty good!

January 2ⁿᵈ, 1994: The Lions beat the Packers 30-20 to win the Central title! Green Bay had five turnovers.

January 8ᵗʰ, 1994: Hey, didn't we just play the Packers? This time it's in the playoffs. We all remember this one: we lose a heartbreaker (has that ever happened before?). 28-24 to Green Bay. Sanders returns and runs for 169 yards. This game would see a 101-yard TD on an interception return by the Packers. A 40-yard TD pass to a wide-open Sterling Sharpe (did someone miss his coverage, perhaps?) with 55 seconds left, ends the season in typical depressing fashion. There's always next year.

September 4ᵗʰ, 1994: The Lions beat Atlanta 31-28 in OT. A Scott Mitchell TD pass to Anthony Carter with 30 seconds left to tie. Hanson kicks a 37-yard FG for the OT win.

September 11ᵗʰ, 1994: Vikings 10-3; the Lions get two first downs and 29 yards in the first half. They hold Minnesota to one 1st down and 59 yards in the second half.

September 19ᵗʰ, 1994: The Lions beat Dallas 20-17 in OT on Monday night. Sanders runs for 194 yards. Detroit has two field goals blocked at the end of regulation and the start of OT, but they prevail on a 44-yard FG with 32 seconds left in OT. One of the great wins of all time!

October 30ᵗʰ, 1994: The Lions 28-25 over the Giants in OT. We set an NFL record by being the only team to ever win three OT games in a season.

November 6ᵗʰ, 1994: The Packers 38-30; four first half turnovers by Detroit. Dave Krieg rallies the Lions back from

38-14 starting in the fourth, but falls short on downs at the Green Bay 15-yard line as time runs out.

November 13th, 1994: Detroit beats Tampa 14-9. Sanders runs for 237; 200 of those in the second half—wow!

November 20th, 1994: The Bears win by holding the ball an amazing 44:12.

December 10th, 1994: The Lions beat the Jets 18-7 as Chris Spielman sets the record for most tackles by a Lion with 166. He is a pure athlete who has won the hearts and respect of Lions fans. I never understood why he left the team a few years before an injury ended his career.

December 17th, 1994: Detroit beats the hated Vikings 41-19—take that, evil empire! Barry Sanders has his sixth run of 60 yards or more this season; can you imagine?

December 31st, 1994: It's playoff time, aren't you excited? Packers 16-12 as Sanders is held to -1 yard on 13 carries (how could that be?). Detroit gains 58 yards and two first downs in the opening half. Herman Moore catches a pass for what appears to be a go head touchdown, but it is ruled out of the end zone. Darn, we were so close. Wait until next year?

September 5th, 1995: Steelers 23-20. A 31-yard field goal as time runs out wins it after Detroit tied the score with three minutes left. The Lions had four interceptions.

September 17th, 1995: Arizona 20-17 as the Cardinals score 14 points in the fourth to overcome a 17-6 Lions lead. Detroit has 15 penalties and loses two fumbles by Sanders. The Lions record seven sacks.

September 25th, 1995: Detroit 27-24 over the 49'ers, who hit the upright on a 40-yard field goal attempt and miss as time runs out.

October 22nd, 1995: Time for my birthday present! Redskins 36-30 in overtime as Washington beats Detroit for the 15th time in a row. Isn't that hard to do? Washington kicks a field goal as time expires to force overtime. The Lions are intercepted four times; the final one in OT for a touchdown and the Redskin win. The Redskins' streak reminds me of the Vikings' streak from the 1970s.

November 12th, 1995: Detroit 27-24 over Tampa. Fontes becomes the coach with the most wins in Lions history with 56, breaking George Wilson's record of 55 wins. Isn't it amazing that since 1934 no coach has ever won more than 55 games before today?

November 23rd, 1995: The Lions 44-38 over Minnesota. Scott Mitchell sets a new Lions record by passing for 410 yards, breaking Bobby Layne's 374-yard record from 1950.

December 10th, 1995: Detroit 24-17 over the Oilers. Mitchell breaks Bobby Layne's record of 26 touchdown passes in a single season.

December 17th, 1995: The Lions 44-0 over Jacksonville. Moore and Perriman both catch over 100 passes each throughout the season—the first time ever in NFL history.

December 23rd, 1995: The Lions 37-10 over Tampa; the first seven-game winning streak for Detroit since 1962.

December 30th, 1995: On to the playoffs with our seven-game winning streak. We are unstoppable, right? Wrong! Eagles 58-37 in the highest scoring playoff game in history. A total collapse when it counts! Seven Lions turnovers, including six interceptions. Philadelphia was up 51-7 as Rodney Peete (hey, wasn't he on our team? That's not fair) goes 17-25 for 270 yards and three touchdowns. Maybe he wanted to send a message to Detroit for trading him. It was Detroit's third straight playoff appearance and third straight exit in the first round. When it counts the most.... Happy new years from your Lions.

APPENDIX E
Season Recaps: 1996-2000

September 1ˢᵗ, 1996: A gut-wrenching 17-13 loss to the Vikings. The Lions have five turnovers. Herman Moore becomes the all-time touchdown leader for Detroit with 36 (that doesn't seem like very many, does it?). Mitchell's fourth interception stalls the final drive at the Vikings' 11-yard line.

October 27ᵗʰ, 1996: Happy birthday! Giants 35-7 with two interception returns for touchdowns.

November 17ᵗʰ, 1996: Detroit 17-16 over Seattle. The Seahawks miss a 42-yard field goal as time expires. It can happen to anyone!

November 24ᵗʰ, 1996: The Bears 31-14; Sanders records his eighth 1,000-yard season in a row—the first NFL player to do so.

November 28ᵗʰ, 1996: The Chiefs win 28-24. Detroit leads 24-21 and KC drives the final eight minutes before scoring the winning touchdown.

December 8ᵗʰ, 1996: The Vikings 24-22. Sanders scores a late touchdown, but the Lions miss the two-point conversion to tie.

December 23ʳᵈ, 1996: A disappointing season ends with a 49'ers win, 24-14. Like usual, the only good news is Sanders running for 175 yards and his third rushing title. Wait until next year?

August 31ˢᵗ, 1997: The Bobby Ross era begins with a 28-24 win over Atlanta.

October 5ᵗʰ, 1997: Buffalo 22-13. Sanders is tackled for a safety with under two minutes left when the score is 13-13.

October 12th, 1997: Detroit 27-9 over Tampa. Sanders runs for 215 yards and two TDs. He becomes the first player in NFL history to have two runs for 80 yards in the same game.

October 19th, 1997: An early birthday present: the Giants 26-20 in overtime. The Lions score a TD with two minutes left, but the Giants win the coin toss for OT and throw a 68-yard TD on the third play of OT. Game over!

November 2nd, 1997: Packers 20-10. Detroit 14-10 at the half. The Lions are scoreless in the second half as the Packers pick off four Lions passes for INTs.

November 9th, 1997: Redskins 30-7, winning their 16th straight over Detroit—"I Can't Believe It!" Washington has the ball for 40 minutes. Sanders moves past Tony Dorsett for third all-time rushing.

November 23rd, 1997: The Lions 32-10 over the Colts. Sanders' third run of 80 plus yards in the season, another NFL record!

November 27th, 1997: The Lions 55-20 over the Bears—the most points ever in a regular season game for Detroit; the most points ever given up by a Bears team. Sanders moves into second place all-time rushing, ahead of Eric Dickerson (13,310 yards). Jason Hanson kicks his 23rd straight field goal, also a team record.

December 7th, 1997: A heartbreaking loss to Miami 33-30. The Lions have five turnovers. After scoring a TD, Detroit misses the extra point, trailing 23-22. The Lions tie the game on a 96-yard drive and two-point conversion. With 1:54 left in the game, Miami drives 54 yards and kicks the winning field goal. How many of these can we take? I guess as many as the Lions give us!

December 14ᵗʰ, 1997: Detroit 14-13 over the Vikings. Mitchell leads the team on a 72-yard drive and TD in the final two minutes for the win. Herman Moore has his third consecutive 100-catch season (only Jerry Rice has done this before); Sanders runs for his 13ᵗʰ straight 100-yard plus game, setting another NFL record. The guy is simply amazing and by far the most exciting Lion I have ever seen.

December 21ˢᵗ, 1997: The Lions beat the Jets 13-10. Sanders becomes the third player to ever rush for over 2,000 yards. The Jets end the game on a Lion INT of a half back option pass. Most memorable in this game is the near tragedy with linebacker Reggie Brown after he stopped breathing on the field after a collision. I will never forget that feeling in the Silverdome— many of us thought this young man had died. Was it possible 1 was in the stands watching a second NFL player die? I never thought it would be possible after the sad day with Chuck Hughes. Thank God Brown was okay, even though his NFL career ended that day.

December 28ᵗʰ, 1997: The playoffs; how exciting, right? Wrong! The Lions' fourth playoff appearance in the past five years ends the same way they all have—with a loss, as Tampa takes it 20-10.

September 6ᵗʰ, 1998: A new season, a new hope. Packers 38-19. Terry Fair has a 101-yard kick return for a TD, but the Packers match it on the next play with a 100-yard return of their own—the fourth time in history this has occurred. Sanders' 14-game streak of 100 yards rushing is snapped as he runs for 70 yards.

September 13ᵗʰ, 1998: The Bengals beat Detroit 34-28 in OT in heart-wrenching fashion. Have we heard this term before?

Sanders makes a TD with 1:52 left to tie. Spindler blocks a 48-yard field goal to force overtime. A 58-yard interception return for a TD ends the game in OT.

October 4th, 1998: The Bears 31-27. Detroit leads 27-10 starting the fourth. Chicago has five fumbles (aren't you supposed to win when you get five turnovers?). Batch throws his first TD pass 98 yards to Morton. We get to the Bears' 15-yard line, but holding brings us back, ending the Lions' chances.

October 15th, 1998: Detroit 27-20 over the Packers. Batch has 11 straight completions, the youngest QB to achieve this since 1992. His 84.2 rating is the highest for a rookie since 1960. Sanders marks his 25th time running for 150 yards; he has his 15th run of his career of 50 yards plus—both NFL records.

October 25th, 1998: I can't wait to see what the Lions give me for my birthday present this year! Vikings 34-13; Lions lead 13-10 at halftime—doesn't that mean we were shut out in the second half? How come the games have to last so long?

November 1st, 1998: The Cardinals 17-15. Isn't this the game with the controversial two-point conversion try? Detroit has six turnovers.

November 8th, 1998: The Eagles 10-9; this game represents many of the worst frustrations that fans have faced over the years with the Lions. The winning field goal is good, even though it hits Spindler's forearm and went through. The final drive for the Lions stalls at the 39-yard line after four Detroit penalties (two holding, one false start, and an illegal pass). The 58-yard attempt by Hanson is no good—game over! The silver lining in the disappointing loss is Sanders reaching 1,000 yards for the 10th straight year. I'm sure I would have snapped many years earlier if not for Barry Sanders.

November 26ᵗʰ, 1998: Detroit 19-16 over the Steelers in OT. The Steelers tie as time runs out to force OT. Detroit wins the coin toss, but Bettis later says he correctly called tails and the ref didn't hear him. Strange things happen when the Lions are involved. Detroit kicks a FG to win in OT.

December 14ᵗʰ, 1998: The 49'ers 35-13 on Monday night. San Francisco rushes for 328 yards.

December 20ᵗʰ, 1998: Atlanta 24-17. The Lions hold a 17-10 lead starting the fourth (why can't the game be shorter?). Moore becomes the fastest receiver to gain 600 receptions (118 games). Does this mean we aren't going to the Super Bowl? See you guys next year!

September 12ᵗʰ, 1999: Detroit 28-20 over Seattle. The first opening road win since 1986. The Lions lead 25-7 at the half.

September 19ᵗʰ, 1999: The Lions 23-15 over the Packers. It's the first opening day sellout at home since 1975. How is that possible?

October 10ᵗʰ, 1999: San Diego 20-10. It is 10-10 at the half; Detroit is sacked six times and has two turnovers. A 42-yard TD return of a fumble in the fourth is the difference.

October 17ᵗʰ, 1999: Detroit 25-23 over the Vikings: The Lions lead 19-0 at the half. Is it me or is there a pattern of the Lions playing poorly in the second half? Gus Frerotte drives 43 yards in the final 1:40 to set up Hanson's winning field goal with seven seconds left; it is Hanson's sixth FG of the day.

October 24ᵗʰ, 1999: The boys come through for my birthday, beating Carolina 24-9. The Lions defense holds the Panthers to three FGs with five possessions inside the Lions' 5-yard line. Now there is some defense!

November 7th, 1999: Detroit beats the Rams 31-27. Frerotte's TD pass with 28 seconds left is set up by a fourth and 26 first down. Ron Rice intercepts Kurt Warner to end it.

November 14th, 1999: Arizona wins 23-19: The infamous two-point controversy! Detroit comes back from 23-7. Frerotte throws for 375 yards; the first two-point try comes at 23-13. At 23-19, another two-point try fails. Boss Ross is second guessed for not taking the point and pulling to within a field goal. The Lions' final drive stalls at the Cardinal 10-yard line as time runs out.

November 21st, 1999: The Packers 26-17; the Lions lead at the half 17-12 (why so many poor second half performances? I say it's coaching).

November 25th, 1999: Detroit 21-17 over Tampa. The Lions lead 21-0 late in the first half; we have never had the killer instinct to put teams away when they are down.

December 5th, 1999: Detroit 33-17 over the Redskins, breaking our 16-game losing streak to Washington! Hanson kicks four field goals for the 10th time in his career. Two are from 50 plus yards; he becomes only the second kicker in NFL history to kick two 50-yard field goals in a game in two different games. Although this is a great accomplishment, and Hanson is a fantastic kicker, it means the Lions have problems scoring touchdowns, doesn't it?

December 12th, 1999: A gut-wrenching 23-16 loss to Tampa—how many times have we used the term "gut-wrenching"? I think it sums up the past 47 years! Detroit leads this one 10-7 at the half and 16-9 early in the fourth. The Lions run a kickoff back to the Tampa 14-yard line. Oops! An illegal block takes it away. "I don't coach them to play that way."

December 25ᵗʰ, 1999: Merry Christmas. Denver 17-7; the Lions rush for 32 yards. Where is Barry Sanders? Oh, I forgot, he snapped and couldn't take it anymore, retiring from football this past training camp. We miss you, Barry.

January 2ⁿᵈ, 2000: We move into a new century. This will surely inspire our Lions. What? Vikings 24-17; their fourth loss in a row even though they clinched their sixth playoff birth since the 1990s. (Hey, they won one of them.)

January 8ᵗʰ, 2000: Washington 27-14. Rice has a 94-yard TD return on a blocked field goal. Is this the start of another 16-game losing streak to the Redskins?

September 3ʳᵈ, 2000: The Lions 14-10 over the Saints; 439 total yards for both teams; 95-yard TD return by Desmond Howard. The Lions botch the snap on a 29-yard field goal ("I don't coach them that way"); the Saints get to the Lions' 29 as time runs out.

September 10ᵗʰ, 2000: The Lions 15-10 over the Redskins; five Hanson field goals; four interceptions for Detroit. Fair INT with 49 seconds left at the Lions' 20 to seal the win.

September 24ᵗʰ, 2000: Detroit 21-14 over Chicago; the first time since 1980 the Lions win their first two on the road (that's pretty sad). Five turnovers by the Bears; Lions 14-0 at the half, but the Bears tie 14-14; Lions win on a 91-yard drive, taking 8:37 for a TD.

October 8ᵗʰ, 2000: The Lions 31-24 over the Packers. Detroit leads 24-6 at the half. Green Bay has five turnovers; two late INTs seal it for Detroit.

October 19ᵗʰ, 2000: The Lions 28-14 over Tampa. It's 11-11 at the half (first time in NFL history); four Tampa turnovers.

October 29ᵗʰ, 2000: A belated birthday present—the Colts 30-18 over Detroit. Indianapolis has five turnovers, but leads at the half 23-0 (how is that possible?).

November 5th, 2000: Miami 23-8 over the Lions. The Dolphins jump off to a 14-0 lead early after recovering an onside kick after their opening TD. It's 14-0 before Detroit touches the ball (bad start to a game). Batch leaves the game with a concussion; Bobby Ross quits after this one.

November 12th, 2000: The Moeller era begins with a 13-10 win over the Falcons. A Hanson 44-yard field goal with 30 seconds left wins it.

November 19th, 2000: The Lions 31-21 over the Giants. Detroit leads 28-0 early in the third. Westbrook has a 101-yard INT for TD.

December 10th, 2000: The Packers 26-13, with five Lions turnovers. Detroit gets back to 12-10 down, but a six-play, 80-yard drive gives the Packers a 19-10 lead (how many times have the Lions scored big TDs to get back in a game, just to have the defense let up a TD on the very next drive?).

December 17th, 2000: The Lions beat the Jets 10-7 when Hardings recovers a Stuart fumble in the end zone for their only TD. The Jets miss a 36-yard field goal with 12 seconds left to end it.

December 24th, 2000: The game that will be remembered forever! The Lions need a win to go to the playoffs, and lose to the Bears 23-20 when Paul Edinger kicks a 54-yard field goal with two seconds left (ouch!). It's another gut-wrenching loss. Detroit had the 10-0 lead in this one—with two minutes left, Detroit recovers a Bears fumble in Chicago territory, but Stoney Case (in for Batch who leaves with a rib injury) could not move the team. Detroit settles for a 26-yard field goal to tie. Case fumbles on the last drive to set up the winning kick. Mr. Ford might snap over this one!

APPENDIX F

Season Recaps: 2001-2003

September 23rd, 2001: Marty Mornhinweg is in for a rough two years—Cleveland 24-14. Ty Detmer throws seven interceptions and the Lions have 15 penalties.

October 8th, 2001: The Rams 35-0.

October 14th, 2001: The Vikings 31-26; the Lions come back from 31-6 down. They get to the Viking 20-yard line as time runs out.

October 21st, 2001: The Titans 27-24; Detroit ties with 1:18 left, but a field goal with 10 seconds left wins it for Tennessee; I guess the defense couldn't hold.

October 28th, 2001: The Bengals 31-27. The first offensive play for Cincinnati is a 96-yard TD run by Corey Dillon. Not a good start.

November 11th, 2001: Tampa 20-17; it was another heartbreaking loss. Detroit tied the game 17-17 with 1:54 left, but you guessed it—the defense can't hold. A 35-yard field goal with four seconds left ends it.

November 18th, 2001: Arizona scores 24 in the fourth to win. Batch is 36-62 for 436 yards; both Lions' records.

November 22nd, 2001: The Lions nearly pull off a fourth quarter, 16-point deficit but fall 29-27 to the Packers. A Lions TD and recovered on side kick with 1:17 left, but the two-point conversion is missed.

December 2nd, 2001: The Bears win when Hanson misses a 40-yard field goal with 24 seconds left for the tie.

December 9th, 2001: After a 0-12 start, the Lions lose another heartbreaker to Tampa 15-12. Tampa scores a TD with 45 seconds left for the win. Mike McMahon's first start.

December 16th, 2001: The Lions' first win of the season! They beat the Vikings (take that, you bastards!) and keep Minnesota out of the playoffs.

December 23rd, 2001: The Steelers 40-7; David Sloan catches his sixth TD pass of the year, which ties him with Charlie Sanders for the most TDs in a year for a tight end. That's not very many to be a record, is it?

January 6th, 2002: Thank God this season is over. If we, the fans, feel this way, you can imagine how the players feel! The Lions 15-10 over Dallas; the last game at the Silverdome. Johnnie Morton catches his 35th TD pass, tying him for second most ever by a Lions receiver. That's not very many over a career, is it?

September 22nd, 2002: Another season, another loss. The Packers 37-31 for the first game at Ford Field. Harrington's heroics fall short as a pass is dropped in the final seconds.

October 13th, 2002: The Vikings 31-24. Minnesota scores 21 in the second half for the win.

October 20th, 2002: The Lions 23-20 over the Bears. The headline reads, "Stewart Shows Lions Are Not So Cowardly." I knew this team had something in common with the Wizard of Oz.

November 3rd, 2002: The Lions 9-7 over the Cowboys. Detroit kicks a winning field goal with 48 second left.

November 24th, 2002: A famous day in Lions history. Marty takes the wind at Chicago in overtime. Detroit never touches the ball, Bears 20-17.

December 15th, 2002: Tampa 23-20. The "Lions slept early," but come back to make it close. Harrington is being treated for an irregular heartbeat.

December 29th, 2002: The Vikings 38-36; a McMahon TD pass with 13 seconds left, but the two-point conversion is no good. Darn, they were so close again! When the conversion fails, "the heart of the Lions is sunk." Mornhinweg says, "The team is primed to make a run, but it's still a handful of players away." The bar is high. He might be in trouble.

September 7th, 2003: The Lions 42-24 over the Cardinals. The Mariucci era begins on a high note. Don't get too excited dedicating the game ball to Mr. Ford after the game; the leading rusher for the Lions gets 44 yards, the leading receiver gets 38 yards. It is the best rookie receiver performance since 1947. Anquan Boldin has 217 yards. Mariucci says it is an emotional day. There will be more to come!

September 14th, 2003: The Packers 31-6. A 64-yard TD run on the second play of the game by Green Bay.

September 28th, 2003: Denver 20-16 over the Lions. The Lions lose their 18th straight road game. Detroit scores the apparent game-tying touchdown in the fourth but misses the point after due to a bad snap (haven't we heard this one before?). Denver wins on a 41-yard field goal with 3:13 left. Guess we didn't do well on the last drive.

October 5th, 2003: The Cowboys 38-7 over Detroit. The Lions open the scoring on a 69-yard TD fumble return by Bly. I guess they didn't do too well after that.

October 26th, 2003: My birthday! The Bears 24-16 over the Lions. The Lions score with 53 seconds left and appear to recover the onside kick. Darn, there is a penalty for an illegal touch before 10 yards. We were so close! Do you think they would have scored, converted a two-point play, and won in overtime? Maybe not.

November 9th, 2003: Detroit 12-10 over the Bears. Hanson kicks four field goals; Detroit rushes for 12 yards. Our receiver Reggie Swinton leads the team in rushing with nine yards.

November 23rd, 2003: The Vikings 24-14, Minnesota scores 17 points in a 45-second span in the fourth. That can't be good.

November 27th, 2003: The Lions 22-14 over the Packers. It's so sad that the Lions website says, "At 4-8, they have surpassed their win victory totals each of the past two seasons." Bly intercepts two and forces a fumble.

December 14th, 2003: The Chiefs win 45-17. KC scores on seven of their first eight possessions and have a total of 521 yards. The Lions tie the all-time NFL record for consecutive road losses with their 23rd straight. See, we are special!

December 21st, 2003: A proud day in Lions history. The record 24th loss in a row on the road. Detroit has eight 1st downs and 106 yards of offense.

December 28th, 2003: The Lions beat the Rams 30-20. Mariucci tells the team early in the week to "just put one game together"; now it is clear why he makes $5 million a year. It is the first time they score over 23 points since the opening game against Arizona. Bly becomes the first Lion to start the Pro Bowl at corner since 1977. The website concludes by saying that "the Lions carved out a program-changing 30-20 win in the last game against the Rams—shunning the Rams' quest for home field advantage throughout the playoffs." Program changing? Let's see! (Source: www.DetroitLions.com)

Author Bio

BARRY SCHUMER WAS BORN IN Detroit, Michigan, and has been a lifelong Lions fan. He lives in Ann Arbor with his wife, Zoe. He has a son, a daughter, and three grandsons. Barry is a clinical social worker/therapist and this is his eighth book.

You can contact him by email at:
schumerbarry1@gmail.com.

www.ingramcontent.com/pod-product-compliance
Lightning Source LLC
Chambersburg PA
CBHW021621120626
46545CB00001B/334